OPENING DAY

OPENING DAY

Cleveland, the Indians, and

a New Beginning

Jonathan Knight

The Kent State University Press · Kent and London

Frontis: With elements of Fenway Park, Wrigley Field, and League Park mixed together, the interior of Jacobs Field is more intimate and cozy than anything Cleveland baseball fans had ever experienced. (*Akron Beacon Journal*)

© 2004 by The Kent State University Press, Kent, Ohio 44242

All rights reserved

Library of Congress Catalog Card Number 2004000681

ISBN 0-87338-815-1

Manufactured in the United States of America

08   07   06   05   04   5   4   3   2   1

Library of Congress Cataloging-in-Publication Data

Knight, Jonathan, 1976–

Opening day : Cleveland, the Indians, and a new beginning / Jonathan Knight.

p.   cm.

Includes bibliographical references.

ISBN 0-87338-815-1 (pbk. : alk. paper)

1. Cleveland Indians (Baseball team)

2. Jacobs Field (Cleveland, Ohio)

I. Title.

GV875.C7K55 2004

796.357'64'0977132—dc22

2004000681

British Library Cataloging-in-Publication data are available.

For Zachary

"The Yankees cannot lose."
"But I fear the Indians of Cleveland."
—*The Old Man and the Sea*

CONTENTS

PREFACE AND
ACKNOWLEDGMENTS

On April 4, 1994, as the Indians prepared to take the field to consummate a sparkling new era of Cleveland baseball in the first-ever game at Jacobs Field, I was busy trying to sneak out of English class to see it.

I was a high school junior, so naturally I felt that I'd learned everything I possibly could, both in English and life in general. More importantly, the Indians—*my* Indians—were about to take part in a wildly historic moment. After sixty years of residing at Cleveland Stadium (which, for baseball at least, had held all the personality and charm of the Texas School Book Depository) the Indians were now going to get to play in a virtual crystal palace. Needless to say, it was a momentous day for Cleveland.

And here I was stuck in this little room in Beavercreek, Ohio, with a bunch of other high school juniors, still glowing over having conquered and pillaged the ACT. Worse still, we were in the middle of a "group thing." You remember those. The teacher split the class into groups of four for some asinine little project. One person in your group hadn't really read the book you were supposed to discuss, and one person just didn't work well with others. So it was up to the other two to decide which one was actually going to do the work. I'd already lost the toss that day and knew I'd be the one doing the "group project" at home that night.

So as my classmates debated and bartered in a classroom that better resembled an Arabian street market, I went to sharpen my pencil (which was mechanical), took a quick glance to make sure the teacher wasn't looking, and slyly slipped out the door. I retreated down the hall to the yearbook room, where I would be spending the next and final period of the day, and found salvation by flipping on the television set there.

I'm not proud of this little story, but I think it demonstrates the gravity of the Indians' first game at Jacobs Field. It was big enough for me to resort to truancy—a first in my academic career. I suppose that's why I wrote this book.

(Because of the importance of that game, I mean, not to make amends for missing the last fifteen minutes of English class that day.)

Seriously, I think I wrote this book because I felt it needed to be written. The Indians' woes prior to the Jacobs Field era had been extremely well documented, and it seems that everybody was tuned in for the glory years that followed through the 1990s. But I never felt that that moment, that one afternoon, really got the attention it deserved. It was the day the Indians' past, present, and future collided, and much like Ebenezer Scrooge's life following a similar experience, things were dramatically different afterward. However, with apologies to Charles Dickens, I truly believe that the Indians' turnaround was more dramatic, if not better written.

What you are about to read is the story of one game—for my money, the most important single game in the history of Cleveland sports. There may have been bigger ones and better ones, games that won championships, games that will be forever remembered, fondly or painfully. But none signified more change, none represented such a drastic athletic and civic turnaround than this one. It marked the day Cleveland once again adopted the Indians as its own after a four-decade renunciation. And also, I think it was the day that marked the completion of the city's comeback from the "oops-we're-bankrupt-and-our-river's-on-fire" days of the 1960s and 1970s. No question, it was a remarkably dramatic afternoon.

Speaking of drama, I've always been a big fan of plays—not just the ambiance of the theater, but the process and trademarks of the writing. The first thing that fascinates me about theater is the way a good playwright can keep the characters in one setting for two hours and through nothing more than dialogue create an enchanting and compelling drama. I'd like to think of this book as homage to that style of writing—a hybrid between playwriting and sports writing, if you will. Our story revolves around the first game at Jacobs Field on April 4, 1994. That's the backdrop. It will be the locomotive of the narrative, the thread that keeps it moving. We'll go back and forth through history along the way, but like the Kellers' backyard in *All My Sons* or that sultry jury room in *Twelve Angry Men,* sooner or later it will all come back to April 4, 1994, at Jacobs Field.

And wouldn't it have been natural while sitting in the stands that day to think back and reflect on some of the more memorable moments over the past century that had led the city and its team to this point? No doubt fans remembered other openers that, on a smaller scale, represented new beginnings. And in their own way those episodes combine to serve as the Cliff's Notes version of the

Indians' voluminous history. Only after appreciating key moments like those could a fan truly comprehend the significance of April 4, 1994.

Thus, during our journey through that opening game, we'll explore other interludes that, in one way or another, take us along the winding path that led the Indians to Jacobs Field.

The structure of *Opening Day* is very similar to Daniel Okrent's groundbreaking *Nine Innings*, first published in 1985. Okrent takes a run-of-the-mill baseball game between Milwaukee and Baltimore and dissects it beautifully, showing all that occurs on the diamond and in the dugout over the course of nine innings and how much we take for granted either in the stands or by experiencing the game via radio or television. Another inspiration was *Forty-Eight Minutes*, in which Bob Ryan and Terry Pluto do the same for what would otherwise be a ho-hum basketball game between the Boston Celtics and Cleveland Cavaliers in January 1987. We have a new appreciation for a night in the National Basketball Association after 356 pages.

While the foundations of both of those tomes were laid on the "just-another-day-at-the-office" premise, *Opening Day* takes a different approach. April 4, 1994, was anything but a typical day for the Indians and Cleveland in general, as you will discover.

In fact, in honor of the ACT that I hurdled that fateful spring, I offer this homespun analogy: To truly understand the path of reconstruction following the American Civil War, you must understand the implications and aftermath of Abraham Lincoln's assassination. Similarly, to fully appreciate the Indians' renaissance of the late 1990s, one must comprehend the significance of the origin and opening of Jacobs Field, encompassed by its first game.

The term *opening day* carries so much meaning in the lexicon of sports. It represents a fresh start, a clean slate. It's a time when the disappointments of last year mean nothing, and a new and glorious future beckons, filled with the boundless potential one can only truly believe on opening day. Sometimes on the ninety-plus Indians' opening days prior to the christening of Jacobs Field that optimism was justified, but usually it was not. On April 4, 1994, the Indians and the city of Cleveland together experienced a true opening day, one in which the past was as forgotten as the winter just endured and the future was as clear and bright as the cloudless spring sky above.

Even a high school junior would have to agree that it had the makings of good baseball—and even better theater.

• • •

Not only does 2004 mark the tenth anniversary of the opening of Jacobs Field, but it is also the tenth anniversary of the original idea for this book. The inspiration swirled through the screen windows of my grandparents' living room in Brunswick, Ohio, on a stormy June evening in 1994 as I laid on couch cushions on the floor seeking sleep but not finding it. The concept struck like much of the lightning that had scorched through the Cleveland area that night, and I immediately pulled out a notebook and started an outline. Believe it or not, the final product is more or less framed exactly the way it was originally laid out that summer night, although the first word wasn't written for almost four years.

And between then and now there were many changes, many ups and downs, and a lot of contributions for which I am eternally grateful.

First and foremost, I must thank my friend and personal editor extraordinaire, Phil Neal, who helped rescue this manuscript from its desk-drawer grave. Although he is not a big baseball fan, Phil helped sand this thing until it was finally ready for public consumption. Thanks again, Splinky.

A couple of years earlier, a generic e-mail I'd sent requesting advice from well-known Indians' scribe Terry Pluto resulted in a phone call from Mr. Pluto himself. He helped point me in the right direction and gave me the shot of adrenaline I needed to get the ball rolling. "Well," my bride-to-be said after I hung up the phone, "you have to write it now."

And speaking of the woman who would become my wife, I must also thank Sara for her endless encouragement and patience that I'm convinced only spouses of writers can fully understand. She'll always be the cleanup hitter in my lineup.

Naturally, I extend thanks to the Kent State University Press, not only for once again agreeing to print something I'd written, but for not batting an eye and deciding to shift into a proverbial two-minute offense to ensure this would hit the shelves in time for the Jake's tenth anniversary. Acquiring Editor Joanna Hildebrand Craig and Managing Editor Kathy Method were, not surprisingly, wonderful to work with, and it was sort of fun seeing how fast we could get things done. But, for the good of your stomach lining and blood pressure, I wouldn't recommend it.

A hearty thanks to the *Akron Beacon Journal* and Susan Kirkman, assistant managing editor for photography, graphics, and presentation, for allowing us to use some of their wonderful photographs from that fateful first opening day at Jacobs Field. Thanks also to Joan Klaas at the *Plain Dealer* for finding the photograph of Bill Clinton. We also tapped into the seemingly endless vault of images in the *Cleveland Press* Collection at the Cleveland State University Library, a true treasure of Northeast Ohio history. Joanne Cornelius found a handful of good shots in two shakes of a lamb's tail, which fit right in with our hurry-up publication schedule.

Another oasis was the Ohio Historical Society's Archives and Library, which played a major role in the researching process, as did the Columbus Metropolitan Library. To me, microfilm is the vital substance of life.

Thanks also must be extended to the sports staffs of the *Plain Dealer* and the *Beacon Journal* for their traditionally wonderful Indians' coverage. But both papers went above and beyond with their work previewing the opening of Jacobs Field, which served as a good starting point for my research.

And though I'm not sure if it had any direct correlation in the writing of this book, I feel obligated to mention the impact of a pair of unique classes I took as a sophomore at Ohio University. Longtime professor Charles Alexander offers a two-part history of American baseball course, one covering the time to 1930 and the other since. (To answer your silent question—yup, liberal arts majors have all the fun). I thought I knew a little something about baseball prior to taking these classes but had a much better understanding of the general timeline of the game and some of its more important sociological impacts. I hope that perspective translates into the following pages.

Finally, I must make a special acknowledgment of my grandfather, Joseph Souhrada, who passed away a few months prior to this book's publication. I suppose my first memories of the Indians originate from him—usually snapping off his small transistor radio while muttering some unpleasant remark about the Tribe. To tell you the truth, I think he was as quietly optimistic about the Indians as anyone, although he coated it with the cynicism of a lifelong Clevelander who lived eighty-six years and experienced just one World Series championship. Underneath, I could tell he still got excited every spring, and now that I look back, it seems appropriate that he and I attended the final opening day at Cleveland Stadium on a cold April afternoon in 1993. That day a torch was passed in Cleveland—and perhaps between us as well.

Thanks, Grandpa. You're safe at home now.

PROLOGUE

With a sharp crack of the bat, the baseball skidded toward shortstop. Omar Vizquel scooped it up and flipped to John McDonald at second base for the third out. The game was over. With a 9-1 victory over the Minnesota Twins, the Cleveland Indians were the 2001 American League Central Division champions.

The Jacobs Field fans, on their feet for the entire ninth inning, roared and cheered—perhaps a bit more passionately than even they would have expected on this warm September afternoon. This was, after all, the Indians' sixth division title in seven years. And it wasn't exactly a dramatic achievement. First, it had been an almost effortless eight-run victory. Also, with a week remaining in the regular season and the Tribe enjoying a comfortable lead, it was just a matter of time before the second-place Twins were mathematically eliminated.

For the previous seven years, making the playoffs had become rather pedestrian for the Indians and their fans. After the first division title in 1995, Clevelanders erupted in a Mardi Gras–type of celebration that they never thought they'd live to see. For the four titles that followed, winning the division sparked about as much excitement for Indians' fans as getting the mail—so much so that the 162-game regular seasons themselves seemed to serve as mere dress rehearsals for October. By 1996 advancing to the postseason was simply expected, and anything less would be considered a crushing disappointment. The 2000 season proved this. A furious late-season rally wasn't enough to overcome the club's midsummer doldrums, and the Indians missed the postseason for the first time since Jacobs Field had opened. Fingers were pointed and blame—even embarrassment—orbited the franchise. A return to the playoffs in 2001 wasn't just expected by Indians' fans, it was demanded. Now their demands had been met.

But that's not what made this celebration so unique, nor what made the fans stay in their seats to watch the players embrace and carouse on the infield after the final out. Although some may not have admitted it at the time, most knew they were witnessing the final chapter of what had been a wonderful story. The winds of change were rising outside Jacobs Field. After watching their team field one of the best squads in baseball and compete for a world title in each of the previous eight seasons, Tribe fans knew things would be different in 2002. A new owner was about to take the team in another direction. A handful of veterans were sure to depart via free agency. And what little promise of youth remained—that which had not been traded away during the previous eight years while searching for the final component to get the team over the hump—wasn't going to be enough to keep the team at this lofty level.

Although the playoffs lay ahead, and a lot of things could happen before the 2002 season began, there was an unspoken understanding circulating through Jacobs Field that day. Both the Indians and their fans knew that the celebration taking place on this sunny Sunday afternoon marked the end of the road. Watching the postgame festivities was like experiencing a rock group's farewell tour or an outgoing president's final address to the nation. Few were in a hurry to leave. Most just wanted to bask in this moment for as long as they could, hoping it would never end.

As the players enjoyed their still somewhat subdued celebration, Indians' center fielder Kenny Lofton came out of the dugout holding a huge, folded-up banner. He carried it over to the group and tried to hand it to pitcher Charles Nagy, who had been with the Indians longer than any of his teammates and whose consistency (and lack of dominance) best personified the team's successful run through the late 1990s. Modest and selfless as always, Nagy refused but was eventually talked into taking the banner. He then led a group of veterans—including Lofton, Vizquel, and first baseman Jim Thome—out across the outfield.

At the fence Nagy and a pair of ballpark employees hooked the banner to a rope and hoisted it up the center-field flagpole. As the pennant crept up the pole, the September breeze caught it and spread it out for the crowd to see: CLEVELAND INDIANS 2001 A.L. CENTRAL DIVISION CHAMPIONS. With Lee Greenwood's anthem "Proud to Be an American" playing over the speakers—the September 11 terrorist attack, which had occurred less than three weeks before, was still fresh in America's minds—the banner reached its summit. The crowd put forth its loudest cheer of the afternoon.

But if one listened carefully—with both ears and heart—he would note those cheers weren't just for beating the Twins that day or for winning the division. A good portion of that ovation was a thank-you to the people, whether still with the team or not, who had made the previous eight seasons so enjoyable. In that moment it seemed that the fans realized how ridiculous *not* getting excited over an Indians' division title would have seemed just a decade earlier. This was a town that had endured much sports suffering over the previous forty years and, consequently, a town that appreciated the good stuff (even if not the *best* stuff) when it came its way, probably more so than any other city in America. That afternoon those in attendance seemed to remember how special—and in the modern landscape of professional sports how *rare*—a run the Indians had enjoyed.

Dark days were on the horizon for this franchise. But even the frustrations that laid ahead were far more preferable than the dank vacuum of the Indians' past. Unlike those days, now there was genuine, well-founded optimism that things would eventually get better. The forthcoming changes would not be a reversion to a history best forgotten but simply a tangent, an inconvenient detour from the path to the success of the future.

After a few more minutes the players wandered into the clubhouse, and the fans began to trickle out of Jacobs Field. Within a half-hour it was just an empty baseball stadium. It was no longer a stage for what may have been the franchise's first real curtain call. The moment had passed. Thus, September 30, 2001, marked the completion of a cycle of athletic success the city of Cleveland would never forget.

Nor, it is hoped, will they forget the beginning.

GATEWAY TO THE JAKE

THE BUILDING OF A BALLPARK

It's hard to say where it all began—to pinpoint the exact moment when Cleveland saved the Indians.

The instinctive answer for longtime Tribe fans lately is May 8, 1990. But much like when trying to excavate the origins of baseball itself (when historical recollection leaps to Abner Doubleday and Cooperstown), to hang the distinction on that date would not be entirely accurate. While the roles of both Doubleday and Cooperstown were myths created by a public relations machine, May 8, 1990, was real. That momentous day was one that changed the Cleveland athletic scene forever. On that day, the Indians were transformed from the most hopeless sports franchise in America to an organization with, if nothing else, optimism for the future. But as is always the case in studying history, nothing is ever as clear-cut as it seems.

On May 8, 1990, Cuyahoga County voters flooded the polls in surprisingly large numbers (49.6 percent of those registered) to voice their opinion on Issue 2, which, if passed, would give the green light to a $344 million tax-funded project called Gateway. Gateway was a simultaneous construction project of both an open-air baseball stadium and a large arena next door. The two facilities would be used primarily as the homes of Major League Baseball's Indians and the National Basketball Association's Cavaliers, respectively. With a large bloc of young voters eager for a downtown renaissance making the difference, Issue 2 passed by the virtual hairs of its chinny chin chin: 198,390 to 185,209 (51.7 percent to 48.3 percent). It ensured that a future would finally be established for the Indians after three decades of strife, with 1994 set as the target for the completion of both projects.

As simple as that sounds, this story doesn't begin there. While there has been constant debate over when and where the blazing of the path to Jacobs Field began, the most appropriate spot in history was probably ten years before the "Jake" opened for business: May 8, 1984, exactly six years before Issue 2 passed.

On that May 8 a similar issue appeared on the Cuyahoga County election ballot. It was a proposal to increase property taxes for the next twenty-five years

Never had one mile seemed like a thousand. A virtual stone's throw from the old Municipal Stadium (upper left) and nestled into downtown Cleveland between Ontario Street, Carnegie Avenue, and East 9th Street is Jacobs Field. (*Akron Beacon Journal*)

to build a multipurpose domed stadium in the Central Market region in the southern portion of downtown Cleveland. Originally proposed by Cuyahoga County Commissioner Vince Campanella, it was envisioned as the eventual home of all three of Cleveland's major professional sports teams: the Indians, the Cavaliers, and the National Football League's Browns. Campanella had hoped to model the project after the Pontiac Silverdome, used by the Lions and Pistons in Detroit, and thought that if Cleveland's dome became reality, the city could potentially host a Super Bowl and bring millions of consumer dollars into the area. (Ironically, Campanella's aspiration was quite similar to the myth surrounding Cleveland's last major sports construction project.) Browns' owner Art Modell, eager to get out of old, musty but mammoth Cleveland Stadium, backed the project once he learned the domed stadium would have at least 70,000 seats.

However, Ohio Governor Richard Celeste opposed the issue, feeling that raising property taxes was not the way to go. He promised voters he would come up with a better plan if they defeated this dome issue. They did, by a two-to-one margin, and a year later Celeste and Cleveland Mayor George Voinovich helped form the Greater Cleveland Domed Stadium Corporation. Over the remainder of the decade the corporation, led by Voinovich, began buying and trading for land in the Central Market area, which was the only downtown location where a stadium could be built. Though the original dome idea was dead, in the years following it became obvious that the Indians would need a new home if they were to stay in Cleveland.

A year after the dome issue was strangled, another proposal, a six-sided dome called the Hexatron, was designed by a local architect. Voinovich nixed the idea, wanting to go in another direction to develop downtown, but the brainstorm did catch the interest of a young member of the Ohio House of Representatives named Jeff Jacobs. Before Voinovich axed the proposal, Jacobs suggested that the Hexatron could be funded by a "sin tax" on tobacco and alcohol products. Less than a year later Jacobs's father, Richard, and uncle David bought the Indians from the estate of the late Steve O'Neill and were less interested in a dome to serve as a home for the team than in a smaller, outdoor park like Wrigley Field or Fenway Park.

City planners still felt that an arena had to be built. Ever since the Cavaliers had moved from the old Cleveland Arena to their palace in the meadows of Richfield in 1974, downtown had been without an attractive venue to hold indoor sporting events or concerts. Though it made the issue tougher to pass, the small outdoor park and the new arena were packaged together on the May 1990 ballot, and proponents put it simply: this could be the foundation for revitalizing the rest of downtown. Led by Cleveland lawyer Tom Chema, County Commissioner Timothy Hagan, and new Cleveland Mayor Michael White, the group decided to use Jeff Jacobs's original idea to fund the Hexatron. A sin tax would raise the price of a pack of cigarettes an extra 4½ cents, add two cents to each glass of beer, and four cents to a 1½ ounce glass of liquor. The excise tax would be set in place August 1, 1990, and would last through 2005. The plan was called Gateway, an obvious reference to what it could be for the city of Cleveland, a bridge to the twenty-first century—but only if it passed.

While many voters hemmed and hawed over the decision, the Gateway group arguably secured victory just days before the election when Fay Vincent, then-commissioner of baseball, was invited to a city council finance-committee meeting. Vincent intimated that if Gateway was defeated, the Indians would eventually leave Cleveland. "Should this facility not be available in Cleveland," he said, "should the vote be a negative one, we may find ourselves confronting a subject we want to avoid."

While that message was powerful, the question still remained: what if Cleveland voters *didn't care* if they lost the Indians? After all, by the 1990s only 37 percent of Northeast Ohioans had been alive when the Indians had won their last American League pennant in 1954. And at one point on election night it appeared as though apathy might take the prize as Issue 2 trailed by 10 percent.

Issue 2's narrow margin of victory demonstrated that threatening to take away a team as incompetent as the Indians had been for the previous thirty years was not as powerful a threat as Gateway supporters had hoped. Still, they had won, and despite the delay a new era was finally under way in Cleveland.

To celebrate, the Indians blew a five-run lead in Minnesota and lost, 6-5.

While the passing of Issue 2 marked the beginning of an exciting new chapter in the history of the Cleveland Indians, it also signaled the start of one of the ugliest situations in the history of the city. Asked by civic officials to wait patiently while Gateway was passed and developed, Art Modell grew increasingly impatient with the city in the next few years as it ignored his efforts to build a new stadium—or revitalize the old one—for his Browns. Feeling jilted by the city officials who gave the Indians everything they'd ever wanted and the Cavaliers a new home they hadn't even asked for, Modell's stubbornness and the city's fumbled relations with him ultimately led to his moving the Browns from Cleveland following the 1995 season. After several years of standing by and eventually adding to the Indians' financial problems, since he was their landlord through the 1970s and 1980s after purchasing Cleveland Municipal Stadium from the city, it seemed Modell couldn't stand to be a part of a community reveling in the Indians' success.

Ironically, in its efforts to redefine the downtown area by building sports palaces and the world-famous Rock and Roll Hall of Fame and Museum (which opened just before the Browns left), the city of Cleveland had lost its franchise with the strongest civic following. The Browns ultimately returned as an expansion team in 1999 in a brand new park built on the site of Cleveland Stadium (demolished in 1996), but the Browns' departure left a scar on the history of Cleveland sports that time may never completely heal.

In 1990, even though Gateway had been passed on the ballot and a bright new tomorrow awaited, it would still be four long years before those dreams became reality, and it would be more than two years until ground was actually broken on the project.

In September 1990 the Gateway trustees appointed Whitley/Whitley Incorporated, Triad Design, Osborn Engineering Company, and HOK Sports Facilities Group to cooperatively design the ballpark. A month later the first model of the complex was revealed to the public, and the expected capacity of the park was estimated to be at around 42,000. In December $145 million worth of tax-exempt bonds to help pay for the remainder of the complex sold out in one day. The following summer the Indians and Gateway officials came to terms on a twenty-year lease for the new park. In October 1991 $16.4 million was raised by the sale of ten-year luxury suite leases. The project was going remarkably smoothly, especially considering no one had picked up a hammer yet.

The implosion of the Cold Storage Building, the final structure to be destroyed in the Central Market region to make way for Gateway, took place on January 12, 1992, and later that month the official groundbreaking ceremony was held for the ballpark, scheduled to open in April 1994. On June 25, with the infield laid out in dirt, temporary bleachers installed, and live television cameras rolling, Indians' pitcher Charles Nagy and former Cleveland hurler Mel Harder—donned in the Indians' uniforms of their respective eras—threw ceremonial first pitches over the spot where home plate would soon be. Just three months later David Jacobs died of pneumonia and sepsis, leaving Richard Jacobs as the primary owner of the team.

As fans drove through downtown to attend the final opening day at Cleveland Stadium in April 1993, the outer structure of the new park was nearly completed and was actually beginning to look like a place to play ball. The site took up twelve acres between Ontario Street, Carnegie Avenue, and East Ninth Street.

During this long construction process, many questions arose about the potentially offensive logo of the Indians, Chief Wahoo. As the final season at Cleveland Stadium began, the Indians announced that the famous neon sign at Cleveland Stadium of the chief preparing to swing a bat would not be moved to the new park. Two months later, despite the team's eventual decision to design new uniforms for its first season at the new park, Richard Jacobs said the team would not be changing its logo. Though the Indians had been one of the worst teams in professional sports for more than thirty years, their logo was one of the most recognized in the world and, as a result, a steady source of merchandising revenue for the franchise.

In January 1994 the team announced that a million tickets had already been sold for the upcoming season in the new park, and before a single pitch was thrown the Indians were assured of their fourth-largest, single-season attendance total. In February the park was reportedly going to be named after Society Bank, which was close to purchasing the naming rights. At the last minute Richard Jacobs paid $10 million for twenty years for the right to name the park. Still, the project had no official name until March 23, twelve days before its first game, when the team announced that the new facility would be called, appropriately, Jacobs Field.

The design of the new park began quite simply, and like most historic moments in baseball, everything started at home plate. Everything that would one day be Jacobs Field emanated from the placement of a seventeen-inch wide piece of rubber. The location of the plate was laid down before any concrete had been poured and followed the template Major League Baseball set forth for all new ballparks. A batter standing at home plate would face northeast, and everything else would orbit home and the direction it faced. As the long construction process droned on between late summer 1992 and spring 1994, the architectural drawings and models slowly became reality.

Lying before the plate was the infield, consisting of natural grass just like at Cleveland Stadium. But the difference between the sod installed at Jacobs Field and what the Indians and Browns had played on at the Stadium was akin to the difference between natural grass and Astroturf. To say the Browns even played on grass isn't particularly accurate. After they shared the playing surface with the Indians through September, the portion of the field inside the twenty-five-yard line at the closed end of the Stadium was all dirt, marking where the baseball infield began. Once the baseball season ended in the first weekend of October (as it always did for the Indians), sod would be laid down on the infield, but it never quite matched the rest of the grass. For the remainder of the football season, the Browns played on infield-outlined (and usually brown) grass. Once the season reached late November, December, and sometimes January, the turf would curl up and die, not to return until May. For several playoff games in the

1980s, grounds-crew members painted the dirt green so that it wouldn't look quite so ridiculous on television.

There would be none of that making-do for the Indians at Jacobs Field. The new sod, laid in September of 1993, was actually a blend of four different Kentucky bluegrasses grown in Indiana for a full year before being transferred. It was planted on twelve inches of sand to anchor the roots. There were two more inches of sandy gravel beneath the sand to help with drainage before the water reached drainpipes eighteen inches below the field. The turf, which was designed to meet United States Golf Association green standards, could drain twelve inches of rain per hour. Also aiding in water reduction (but taking away from some of the natural feel of the playing field) was a brown rubberized surface laid down around the field to serve as the warning track.

The first glaringly obvious quirk in the layout of the field itself was in left field. More appropriately, it was the end of left field: a nineteen-foot wall towering over the outfield 325 feet from home plate, which some began calling "Jacobs's Ladder." Traveling into fair territory from the foul pole, the fence angled outward, then formed a cranny at an angle. Along the straight line of wall that followed was the deepest part of left center at 370 feet from home plate. Another angle formed in straightaway center in the deepest part of the ballpark, 410 feet. That was also the spot where the nineteen-foot wall dropped down to eight feet, creating an interesting dilemma. A high drive to straightaway center could either pound into the nineteen-foot wall or, if two inches to the right, sail out of the park. As the project neared completion, it became evident that those two inches could be the difference between a home run and a long single and quite possibly between victory and defeat.

Ready to bear witness to any of those injustices (or acts of mercy, depending on who's trotting to first at the time), the Indians' relief pitchers were set to have a great view, with the home team's bullpen less than fifty feet from the angle in center. In the pen there were three mounds instead of the traditional two, enabling a trio of pitchers to warm up at once.

The fence remained at eight feet tall through right center (375 feet at its deepest point) and into right, then angled at another cranny about 100 feet from the foul line. The fence continued in front of the visitors' bullpen, which was raised like the home bullpen, 4½ feet from the playing field and nestled in the right-field corner. The distance down the right-field line was 325, the same as down the left-field line, creating bookends of exactitude in the otherwise eclectic outline of the outfield. But that's what the designers were going for and what fans liked to see, especially after witnessing the blandness of Cleveland Stadium and the cookie-cutter mausoleums constructed in the previous quarter-century in cities such as Cincinnati, Philadelphia, Pittsburgh, and Atlanta. As Bob Dyer of the *Akron Beacon Journal* wrote, Jacobs Field was, "Big enough to be exciting, small enough to be intimate. Old-fashioned, yet brand-new. And just a little bit quirky."

While quirkiness by design is a bit less impressive than quirkiness seasoned by history and circumstance, it was clear that the design of the field itself was based in part on baseball monuments like Wrigley Field in Chicago and Fenway Park in Boston. Two features connected with the left-field wall at Jacobs Field made this even more obvious. Although the wall at Jacobs Field was clearly patterned after the thirty-seven-foot Green Monster in Boston, inserted in the padded, green structure was a long, horizontal scoreboard that projected the scores of all the other games going on in baseball that day. The "fenceboard" was divided into three portions: the American League scores were on the left portion, the National League on the right, and a smaller message board in the middle. The message board might occasionally describe highlights of what was going on elsewhere but usually just displayed the names of the teams playing that day at Jacobs Field and the date. Instead of hiring someone to crawl into the wall and slide numbered planks into the appropriate slots like at Fenway, the Jacobs Field fenceboard was controlled electronically.

Atop the nineteen-foot wall in left, homage to Wrigley was paid in four sections of bleachers. Before the park even opened, rumors spread that those just might be the best seats in the park for the average baseball fan. Metal, not wood like at the Stadium, and with backs, at six dollars a seat, the bleachers certainly promised to be the best value in the park. But many who purchased seats in the bleachers could decide to forfeit them for a spot standing on the "Home Run Porch," the concrete patiolike area overlooking left field between the end of the bleachers and the foul pole. Hundreds of fans would watch games from that spot in the years to come, hoping for souvenirs, and the Home Run Porch would turn out to be an accidental innovation that would be nationally recognized and associated with the excitement of Cleveland fans celebrating a home run.

The one downfall of the bleachers was that fans sitting there couldn't really enjoy the most eyecatching portion of the new stadium, the scoreboard. Advertised as the largest freestanding scoreboard in North America (one writer wittily noted that there must have been a bigger one in Japan leaning up against a tree), the $9 million, 120-by-220-foot scoreboard was the most dramatic of all the visible differences between Jacobs Field and Cleveland Stadium. Written in a classy cursive script across the top was "Indians" in red letters outlined in white lights that would be turned on for night games and put on a chase pattern following

each Cleveland victory. The scoreboard was split into three state-of-the-art sections: on the far left was a message board measuring twenty-six feet by thirty-
seven feet, providing information for the fans and featuring animation displays.
Directly beneath the "Indians" script was the actual scoreboard, including the
entire batting team's lineup, up-to-the-minute statistics of the current batter,
and, naturally, the count, the number of outs, and the inning-by-inning display
of the score. On the far right was the giant Sony Jumbotron (also twenty-six-by-
thirty-seven) that, among other things, could provide instant replay for the fans
in the park.

Another interesting feature of the scoreboard was that it could realistically
be struck by a hit ball, a feat virtually impossible and never accomplished at
Cleveland Stadium. It would be three years before anyone did at Jacobs Field—
and that individual pulled it off twice in just over a year.

At the point where the bleachers ended and the wall dropped down in center
field, a huge picnic plaza was built behind the fence for fans to make reserva-
tions and chow down before the game. Shielding the plaza from the field and the
Indians' bullpen were a series of trees. Come the proper time of year, the Indians
were hoping that their grounds crew would be particularly careful about raking
up the leaves in that area of the park. If Jacobs Field was to be the site of television broadcasts in October, the Indians would have to clean up for company.

Just behind the visitors' bullpen in right field was another revolutionary idea:
a spacious play area for children called Kidsland. Packed full of toys and activi-
ties from appropriate sponsors, it was designed for the parents of small children
who came to the game. If a child got fussy or wasn't particularly interested in
whether the manager would give a hitter the green light or the take sign on a 3-
and-0 count, a parent could drop the tyke off at Kidsland. Plus, the parent could
then turn around and still watch the game from the right-field corner.

Staring out at the field from that point, mom or dad could not help but notice
a long structure of glass jutting out of the left-field grandstand, hanging over the
third-base seats. This was the Terrace Club Restaurant. Highlighted by giant glass
windows that stretched ceiling to floor, the Terrace Club was only accessible during games by season-ticket holders or fans sitting in even more ambitious sections
of the park. The Club expected to open to the public for lunch in June on days
when the Indians had no afternoon home game, but before that it would simply
be for those who forked out the most money to attend the ballgame. Of course,
the average baseball fan might not enjoy salmon and oak-fired vegetables or garlic
herb chicken and wine as much as they would hot dogs, popcorn, and beer.

The seats down the outfield lines, which in most parks traditionally offer a perpendicular angle to the action on the field, were angled anywhere from eight to ten degrees inward so that "the crick in your neck by the ninth inning is a little less," according to ESPN's Chris Berman. A large metal sign, shaped like a pennant flapping in the Lake Erie breeze, numerically marked each section.

Even the new seats were beautiful. Painted hunter green to mimic the ocean of outfield grass, the seats were actually two inches wider than their counterparts at Cleveland Stadium, possibly in accommodation of the enthusiasm for ballpark goodies that fans had developed over the last sixty years.

Speaking of baseball delicacies, Jacobs Field also represented the light years stadium food service had come since that day in 1901, at the Polo Grounds, when an ingenious program peddler slapped a German sausage in a bun because the weather was too cold to sell ice cream. In addition to the usual hot dogs and hamburgers, fans could also feast on kosher dogs, Polish sausage, or bratwursts; sandwiches of barbecued pork, steak, chicken salad, roast beef, corned beef, or turkey breast; Italian subs; and garden or Caesar salads. And that's just if they wanted a snack. There was also pizza by the slice, chicken fajitas, burrito supremes, egg rolls, popcorn, and taco salad. Plus, there was a kids' menu featuring favorites like peanut butter-and-jelly sandwiches, cotton candy, and snow-cones. Fans could also have dinner, with choices such as fried chicken, barbecued ribs, teriyaki kabobs, or chicken planks. Naturally there was also dessert: fruit cups, cinnamon rolls, brownies, ice cream, and chocolate eclairs.

And it goes without saying that all sixty-eight varieties of munchies could be washed down with beer: fourteen kinds, foreign or domestic, draft or can, ranging from $3.35 to four bucks. But arguably the most welcome feature of these new-age concession stands (designated as "All-American," "Grill," "Deli," and so on) wasn't what was on the menu, but that fans could stand in line at most of them without missing any action on the field. With many stands located right on the concourse levels, fans simply needed to turn around to see what was happening on the field while they waited for their peanuts and Cracker Jacks.

Grateful visitors to Jacobs Field would discover even more welcome features to the new park in the restroom department. A total of nineteen restrooms for each sex were strewn about the stadium, along with two unisex versions for parents with small children. What's more, the restrooms actually looked as if they'd been designed in the twentieth century. After decades of male fans at Cleveland Stadium going into cattle troughs and female fans endlessly waiting in line (legend had it some who had attended a game in 1978 were still waiting in line the day Jacobs Field opened), fans now no longer needed to worry about a ballgame bathroom trip being a three- or four-inning experience.

A multi-inning wait could be expected, however, for fans wanting to check out the new Indians Team Shop and Museum, located on the main concourse behind the third-base line seats. Inside fans could find anything from hats to t-shirts to sweatshirts to collectibles. And attached to the back of the store was the museum, which included several artifacts dug out of the Indians' sometimes rich-as-chocolate, sometimes runny-as-vinegar, past. Due to fire codes and a simple lack of space, fans would have to wait in line just to get into the team shop during Jacobs Field's inaugural season and for many years thereafter.

Again varying from Cleveland Stadium, Jacobs Field was a triple-deck affair all the way around. Much of the second deck was taken up by luxury suites, 109 in all, around the field's circumference. Luxury-suite holders had a choice: the twelve-seat style or the eighteen-seat Presidential Suite. Each let fans enjoy the games while sitting outdoors in the same green seats as the rest of the crowd or hang out in the loge itself with its kitchen, wet bar, and full-service catering. All in all, it was a great way to watch a ballgame—for a minimum of $3,000 per contest.

For fans who wanted to put out even more for their baseball-viewing experience, there were ten dugout suites down on the field. These suites (the closest of which sat fifty-eight feet from home plate—even closer than the pitcher) were nestled between the end of each team's dugout (which fans could look into through tinted glass on the side wall) and the area directly behind home plate. These suites, targeted for large corporations, had to be purchased for the entire season for $100,000.

Most baseball fans felt that it was ridiculous to have the difference between the cheapest and the most expensive seats in the house to equal the cost of a college education, but the reality was that by the 1990s this was the way the game was played in professional sports. Teams made more money off the yearly rent from the loges, or "skyboxes" as they were sometimes called in arenas, than they usually did on the rest of the seats combined. It was these loges that led to better attendance, more money, more free-agent signings, and usually more victories. By its 125th anniversary in 1994, professional baseball had certainly come a long way from the days of one-coin admission in the nineteenth century.

The other obvious innovative feature at Jacobs Field was the spectacle that was the ballpark's lights. Not horizontally connected and stapled to the roof like at Cleveland Stadium (and at most other ballparks), each section of illuminators stood separately on its own tower and was hung vertically, partially to be unique and partially to help keep outfielders from losing the ball in the lights. Each of the nineteen towers stood 200 feet high and contained 698 metal halide lamps, each of which was computer-aligned to cover an exact spot on the field to keep the light perfectly balanced. It didn't take long before people starting calling them what they looked like: "toothbrush lights."

Ironically most fans would never see some of the most dramatic differences between Cleveland Stadium and Jacobs Field. The new clubhouses were four times bigger and infinitely better than their counterparts at Cleveland Stadium, where Houston Oilers' head coach Jerry Glanville once claimed he would have to use a hammer and nail to hang up his coat. Upon seeing the Jacobs Field clubhouses (each covered with a rich burgundy carpet, including six leather couches, and eight televisions hanging from the ceiling), anyone who had spent time in the Cleveland Stadium locker rooms would think they'd died and gone to heaven. Add forty-nine roomy wooden dressing cubicles, each with its own executive chair, and top-of-the-line weight and aerobic rooms, manager and coaches' suites, a players' kitchen, a video room, and a huge training room, and you had some very happy people.

Spreading the wealth of happiness, the batboys got their own room, and the media interview room seemed to be the size of Rhode Island. Giving a tour for the media shortly before Jacobs Field opened, Indians' vice president of public relations Bob DiBiasio remarked that this new room was big enough to handle the media blitz of a World Series. "Now, that's not a guarantee," he added coyly, "it's just for informational purposes."

Directly behind each dugout sat four indoor batting cages that teams could use for practice before the game if the weather was bad. Pinch hitters could also warm up in them during the game before going up to the dugout. Ironically, of all the new features for the players and coaches in the new structure, these cages would be the only ones that would have an immediate and dramatic impact on the first game at the park.

Probably the most important and impressive visual feature of the new park wasn't anything that was constructed—it was what *wasn't* constructed. No matter where you were in Jacobs Field, you could see some hint of the Cleveland skyline or some architectural reminder of where you were. For example, with the Terminal Tower peeking over the third-deck roof above the third-base line and the Ameritech building towering over the scoreboard in center, there was no doubt, as many writers put it, that while sitting in the Cleveland park you were clearly sitting in Cleveland.

Even the outer construction of the park contained symbolic ingredients of the city it called home. A good portion of the 10,000 pounds of steel used to create Jacobs Field went into the latticelike outer structure that matched the many bridges in the downtown area. Continuing this trend, the vertical lights complimented the high-rise buildings of the city skyline, as well as the industrial smokestacks just outside downtown. The lower foundation of the ballpark, beneath the steel frame, contained seven different kinds of granite and limestone.

Outside there were monuments to the city and its baseball tradition. A ten-foot-tall bronze statue of Indians' pitching great Bob Feller, in mid-delivery, stood outside the East Ninth Street entrance, affectionately called Indians Square. Leading up to the statue were hundreds of bricks laid in the ground with the names of individuals and corporations who paid up to $100 per brick to help fund the stadium. While the Feller sculpture reminded visitors of the Indians' past, twenty-five large banners, measuring 10 feet high and 5½ feet wide, hung along the outer concourse and brought attention to the present. Each banner portrayed a photograph of a current Indians' player and was visible from the streets outside Jacobs Field.

While East Ninth traveled parallel with the right-field fence of the ballpark, Carnegie Avenue ran along the first-base line and intersected with Ontario Street at the main entrance. Marked by a large sign declaring, "JACOBS FIELD: Home of the Cleveland Indians," with its script and coloring matching the scoreboard inside, the main entrance led fans into the heart of the ballpark, right behind home plate at ground level. It was yet another welcome departure from the design of Cleveland Stadium, where fans would enter most ticket gates high above the field.

For better or worse, many critics would compare Jacobs Field to the most recent major-league stadium constructed, Oriole Park at Camden Yards, which opened in 1992. Unlike the new Comiskey Park, which opened in Chicago in 1991, Camden Yards was the first in what would become a long line of "throw-back" ballparks, mimicking the style of the early twentieth-century yards but still state-of-the-art in every way imaginable. Cleveland officials were hoping Jacobs Field would bring something akin to the $52.8 million Camden Yards injected into the Baltimore economy two years before, but at the same time fans had to be aware that Cleveland needed a ballpark of its own, not a carbon copy of another. "I don't believe in replicating what someone else has," Richard Jacobs said as the ballpark neared completion. "I didn't want something out of a file drawer. I wanted to start with a clean piece of paper."

While both stadiums had unusually high sections of outfield wall (in Baltimore it was right, in Cleveland it was left), the only other notable similarity was the structure of both clubs' executive offices, comprised of varying shades of tan brick with numerous windows. At Camden Yards the offices were placed just behind the stands over the right-field wall; at Jacobs Field the offices were on the side of the structure along Ontario Street. However, Camden Yards wasn't the only structure Jacobs Field would be compared to.

For the first time since 1970, when Cincinnati's Riverfront and Pittsburgh's Three Rivers stadiums opened, two new major-league ballparks would be christened in the same season: Jacobs Field and the Ballpark in Arlington, the new home of the Texas Rangers. Unlike the area developers had in which to nestle Jacobs Field, the Ballpark was spread out over 270 acres near the old Arlington Stadium, and the plucky Texans used every last foot. Surrounding the Ballpark were a Six Flags amusement park, a water park, and several other shopping and entertainment venues. There were some similarities to Jacobs Field inside the stadium. Texas's left-field wall was fourteen feet tall and also contained an out-of-town scoreboard. The Rangers also had their own nod to the great baseball cathedrals with a right-field area that mimicked Tiger Stadium and a roof supported by steel posts that, like at Cleveland Stadium, blocked the views of several seats. While the Ballpark and Jacobs Field had a few things in common, in general they were as different as apples and oranges. The *Plain Dealer*'s Tony Grossi wrote, "Cleveland built a ballpark, Texas built a destination." The $189 million price tag for the Ballpark overshadowed Jacobs Field's $169 million.

As Jacobs Field's first opening day drew closer in the spring of 1994, the jury was still out on whether the new yard would be a hitter's or a pitcher's park. The nineteen-foot wall in left field would turn a lot of right-handers' home runs into doubles, but with the wind currents the ball was expected to travel farther. Conversely, the unpredictable wind could also knock down a lot of potential home runs. While Jacobs Field was about a mile away from Lake Erie, and it was expected to be eight or nine degrees warmer than at Cleveland Stadium on any given day, the lake and its wind currents could still have an impact on baseball games in Cleveland. No one would know until the season began whether Jacobs Field would continue on the recent era of the hitter in Major League Baseball or subdue it. Regardless, the park was not the only reason 1994 marked a new era in Indians' history.

For the casual observer it would become clear very early in the new season that the Indians were, if nothing else, in a new era of fashion. The team discarded the old uniforms it had worn throughout much of the 1980s, which were about as bland as Cleveland Stadium. The Indians' home whites now featured the same red "Indians" script that adorned the giant scoreboard at Jacobs Field. The script, like the new ballpark, was designed as a new-age throwback, in this case back to when the Indians last had the team name stitched in script across their chests, from 1946 to 1957. Red piping encircled the collar and ran down the center of the jersey, and it also trimmed the bottom of the sleeves. Just above the trim on the left sleeve was the cartoon logo of Chief Wahoo and, on the right, a patch commemorating the inaugural season at Jacobs Field. Red and navy piping marched down the sides of each leg, while the pants included a red belt with red stirrups and red shoes. On the back the player's name was arched in red lettering trimmed in navy, as was the number just beneath it. The cap for home games, made of a blue base with a red bill and a Chief Wahoo logo on the front, remained the same, but for the newly designed road uniforms, the base and bill were both blue.

"Cleveland" was written on the road uniforms in the same style and color as on the home ones, and it stood out well against the all-gray shirts with navy piping. In addition to navy stirrups and black shoes, the road outfits substituted a patch commemorating the 125th anniversary of professional baseball for the inaugural season patch. For the first time in their history, the Indians also had an alternate home top, designed exactly like the white home shirt, but it was navy with white piping. The alternate jersey was to be worn on special occasions but would not be worn in the first-ever regular season game at Jacobs Field.

The other noticeable change for Indians' fans in 1994 would be realized in the sports pages. Following a season in which the San Francisco Giants had won 103 games and failed to make the playoffs, Major League Baseball was altering its four-division format—which had been in place since 1969—to a six-division setup, with three in each league, for 1994. Both leagues would still have East and West divisions, but two Central divisions were created, and several teams were moved accordingly. In the American League, the Toronto Blue Jays, the New York Yankees, the Baltimore Orioles, the Detroit Tigers, and the Boston Red Sox stayed put in the AL East, while the Indians and Milwaukee Brewers joined the new Central. The Tigers had an opportunity to move to the new division but turned it down. The Indians, however, were eager to get out of what had been (and would remain) one of the toughest divisions in baseball. Joining Cleveland and Milwaukee in the Central were the Chicago White Sox, the Kansas City Royals, and the Minnesota Twins. Remaining in the West were the Texas Rangers, the Seattle Mariners, the California Angels, and the Oakland Athletics.

In the National League, the Cincinnati Reds and the Houston Astros were moved from the West to the Central, as were the Pittsburgh Pirates, the St. Louis Cardinals, and the Chicago Cubs from the East. Staying put in the East were the Philadelphia Phillies, the Florida Marlins, the New York Mets, and the Montreal Expos, while the Los Angeles Dodgers, the San Francisco Giants, the San Diego Padres, and the Colorado Rockies remained in the West. The Atlanta Braves moved from the West to the East.

The new league playoffs would feature the three division champions plus one wild-card team. The first round of play would be a best-of-five-game division series, followed by the traditional best-of-seven in the league championship series and the World Series.

Once the 1993 season was over and construction on Jacobs Field neared completion, the Seattle Mariners were scheduled as Cleveland's first regular-season opponent at the new park. While Seattle would help the Indians write the first page in what many hoped would be a wonderful new chapter in the history of the franchise, this coincidental quirk of scheduling couldn't help but remind longtime fans of an ugly episode from the Indians' past, exactly thirty years before.

Clamoring for a major-league team in 1964 the city of Seattle had done its best to lure the Indians out of Cleveland. Then-owner and general manager Gabe Paul warned city officials that he was seriously considering moving the team to the northwest, especially if Cleveland Stadium wasn't improved dramatically. Seattle officials quietly collected money for potential season tickets and local television and radio stations placed bids for the broadcasting rights. Paul traveled to Seattle, which was the home of a minor-league team in the Pacific Coast League, during the 1964 World Series but soon realized the potential move was not a realistic possibility. The Indians could ill-afford to play in a minor-league ballpark with less than 25,000 seats while they waited four or five years for a new stadium to be built. Similar situations arose in Oakland and Dallas, two more cities eager for Major League Baseball with stadiums under construction but no immediate permanent home. The Indians eventually got the money from Cleveland for the improvements they wanted and announced that they would stay, but the entire incident left a scar that would take time to heal.

Now, nearly three decades later, the story would come full circle. The Seattle Mariners, who began play as an expansion team in 1977, would come to Cleveland, a city with a ninety-three-year-old baseball team on the cusp of wiping out a generation of public-relations snafus and front-office meltdowns. The teams would play on a Monday afternoon, April 4, and after an off day Tuesday would meet again that Wednesday night to complete the brief two-game set. Whether it was looked on as the last chapter of a long, frustrating tale or the first chapter in what appeared to be a glowing new one (or quite possibly the bridge between both), April 4, 1994, would be the point of impact between the Indians' past and their future.

Rarely do moments so anticipated in the world of sports live up to expectation, but without question this one did.

GAMEDAY

Former Indians' pitcher Bob Feller fires a ceremonial first pitch as Ohio Governor Dick Celeste (with bat) and Indians' owner Dick Jacobs look on. (*Akron Beacon Journal*)

President Clinton waves to the crowd on his way to the mound for his ceremonial first pitch. (Gus Chan © 1994 *Plain Dealer*)

It's been said so many times that it's long since become cliché, and it will be repeated in the future until it becomes scripture: opening day is special.

It was true in 1994 even in Cleveland, Ohio, where the beginning of a new baseball season had been anything but a tiding of great joy for the previous thirty-five years. Even when the team was down during all those dank years, huge crowds always found their way into Cleveland Stadium to celebrate the start of a new season. The event alone became a day circled on the calendars of Northeast Ohioans.

The distinction of a home opener in Cleveland was even immortalized as the backdrop for a network television program. In 1992 an entire episode of ABC's post–World War II–era drama, *Homefront,* centered on the Cleveland Indians' 1946 opener. The show, which took place in a fictional suburb of Cleveland called River Run, included a young character named Jeff Metcalf, who was invited to spring training in Florida by the Indians that winter. After several mishaps, he eventually made the team, bringing nearly all of the ensemble characters out to Cleveland Stadium (or in this case, a Hollywood soundstage) to watch their hometown hero. Naturally, the game turned out to be pretty exciting. The Indians trailed the Detroit Tigers, 5-3, with one out and a man on first in the bottom of the ninth, when the disembodied voice of Cleveland manager Lou Boudreau told young Metcalf he would be pinch hitting for a guy named Richardson (who, like Metcalf, was totally fictional). Metcalf strode to the on-deck circle and received a standing ovation as the hometown contingent realized that he could potentially win the game. But before he got the chance, the batter ahead of him grounded into a double play to end the contest.

Although history took a back seat to storytelling in this episode (the Indians actually played in Chicago to open the '46 season and won, 1-0), it showed that opening day was a big part of many people's lives in Cleveland and had been for several generations. 1994 would prove to be no exception.

A more appropriate example of what many realists expected on opening day in 1994 could be derived from another television reference. This one is from a 1984 episode of the sitcom *Family Ties,* which followed the weekly adventures of the Keaton family in Columbus, Ohio. Wanting to go to a baseball game in Cleveland on a summer afternoon with an older boy she had a crush on, youngest daughter Jennifer called the Indians' box office to see if any tickets remained available for that night's doubleheader with the Seattle Mariners. "You have 35,000?" she said next. "I only need two."

Later when she told older brother Alex (played by Michael J. Fox) of her plans to go see the Indians and Mariners, he responded the same way any baseball fan of the 1980s would have. "Whoa," he quipped sarcastically. "A clash of the titans."

But it was no ordinary matchup between the Cleveland Indians and Seattle Mariners on April 4, 1994. After all, how many times had *Good Morning America* and cbs *This Morning* posted live correspondents at the site of a game? Admittedly, the two programs weren't there to report on the excitement surrounding a typical Indians-Mariners game. They were there because of brand-new Jacobs Field, which that afternoon would open its doors for a regular-season game for the first time.

As is customary, much of the media attention for the opening of a new park has nothing to do with baseball. There's the new stadium and everything that makes it unique, the appearance of famous franchise alumni, various special pregame festivities, and, of course, the person who throws out the ceremonial first pitch. In this case, it couldn't have gotten much bigger: the president of the United States, Bill Clinton, would be on hand for the game. The Indians had played before President George Bush when they opened Camden Yards with a loss to the Orioles in 1992, but it would be the first time the Mariners had ever played before the president of the United States. The prime minister of Mongolia had attended a Seattle game in 1993, but that was a far cry from having the leader of the free world in the stands.

"With President Clinton, the most powerful man in the world, coming, everything is different," ballpark operations director Jim Folk told the *Plain Dealer*. "There's a lot of planning and behind-the-scenes things."

For example, when Indians' Vice President of Public Relations Bob DiBiasio checked his phone messages at 5:30 A.M., he had three from the White House trying to solidify the president's schedule. Clinton's morning would begin in Washington, D.C., officiating the annual Easter-egg roll on the White House lawn before flying to Cleveland.

Fifteen minutes after the rendezvous with his answering machine, DiBiasio checked on the three local television teams located on the Home Run Porch in left field preparing for their morning show reports. With crews arriving since 3 A.M., the ballpark's toothbrush lights had been on all night.

At 6:45, about the same time that the two network morning shows were finding outlets for their equipment, an espn truck pulled into Jacobs Field to prepare for its broadcast of the game, which was set to begin at 1:05 P.M. Preparing for Clinton's arrival, the Secret Service, along with several members of a bomb squad, a K-9 team, and sharpshooters, arrived at 8:06. Indians' utility infielder Alvaro Espinoza the first player to arrive, beat the government teams to the park by about forty-five minutes. "Everything I need is here," Espinoza told the *Plain Dealer* about his up-with-the-rooster exuberance. "If I had a king-sized bed here, I wouldn't have to pay rent on an apartment."

Down on the field forty minutes later, a television crewmember wandered a little too far off the rubberized track. "GET OFF THE GRASS!" screamed field-maintenance manager Brandon Koehnke, who had already attended to the turf as if it were a new baby, wiping off the early-morning frost by hand.

By 8:30 most of the Indians had arrived and were lounging around the state-of-the-art clubhouse. They were just in time to see the Secret Service's bomb-sniffing dog go through the Indians' dugout. It didn't uncover any problems.

Batting practice began at 9:58, with Cleveland bullpen coach Luis Isaac tossing the first pitch to Indians' center fielder Kenny Lofton. Lofton wisely checked his swing when he saw about 180 members of the Cleveland Orchestra and Chorus warming up in right field for their performance of the national anthem. They quickly relocated.

At 10:45, with thousands of fans anxiously waiting with their tickets, the gates swung open, and by 11:00 most of the early crowd was in the house. Though it was the first official game at Jacobs Field, it wasn't the initial crowd to maneuver its way inside. In fact, this marked the fourth consecutive day that fans had the opportunity to enter the new stadium.

Their first chance was Friday afternoon, while the Indians were 140 miles away in the Keatons' hometown of Columbus. The Tribe was playing the Cincinnati Reds at Cooper Stadium for the Ohio Cup, a tradition begun in 1989 to add some spice to the end of spring training for both teams and their fans. The Indians had dominated the intrastate series and continued to do so that Friday with an 8-4 win. The game was shown on the Jumbotron television screen on the new scoreboard, and fans were welcome to come inside and watch. On Easter Sunday afternoon fans were invited (for a small admission price) to watch the team work out, with the proceeds of the entry fee going to Cleveland Indians' charities.

But the big event of the weekend brought more people out than Friday and Sunday combined. The Indians returned from Columbus for the first official (and yet still *un*official) event at Jacobs Field—an exhibition game with the Pittsburgh Pirates on Saturday afternoon. Packed into the new ballpark were 41,326 fans, more to get a glimpse of it rather than to watch the team.

Something television viewers caught a glimpse of was Pittsburgh manager Jim Leyland smoking a cigarette in the dugout during the game, as was his custom. It was a truly ironic sight in the first event held at a brand-new, no-smoking ballpark funded by a tax on tobacco products.

The fans' tepid steps toward optimism for the team's chances in 1994 hit a snag on Saturday as the Indians seemed to prove what many already expected: they would be shaky and inconsistent. Dressed in their new special occasion blue tops, the Tribe jumped to a 4-3 lead in the eighth when a Mark Lewis double scored Wayne Kirby. But in the top of the ninth, trying to close out the game, reliever Eric Plunk walked home the tying run. Then, on a routine ground ball in the tenth, a wild throw by Cleveland third baseman Jim Thome drew first baseman Paul Sorrento off the bag and set up the Pirates' go-ahead run, which scored on a sacrifice fly. A moment later another run scored when Cleveland's rookie right fielder, Manny Ramirez, couldn't catch a routine fly ball. The Indians lost, 6-4, and it seemed to be a prelude of things to come.

Still, it was a sparkling day for the franchise. The early verdict on the new park from the fans and media was that it was clearly a hit. "It's so nice, I thought we were on the road," Sorrento had said.

Outside, scalpers were selling tickets for the exhibition contest for up to $80. Inside, the Team Shop collected $50,000 in sales, and by midafternoon Jacobs Field had already been the site of one wedding proposal. But on the field there was genuine reason for concern.

First, the bullpen had blown a lead and lost the game. Even after lefty Russ Swan beat out fellow southpaw Brian Barnes and righty Jason Grimsley for the final spot in the pen in spring training, several questions still remained. Former New York Yankee Steve Farr, signed as a free agent in February, was expected to be the closer, but all the other roles were left up for grabs. Plunk, Jeremy Hernandez, and Derek Lilliquist had all contributed in 1993 from the bullpen, which Jose Mesa now grudgingly joined after having been the Indians' most durable starter the year before.

While the relief corps looked shaky, the good news was that it didn't need to be the anchor of the team. For the first time in nearly five years, the Indians had assembled a quality starting pitching rotation of Dennis Martinez (signed as a free agent from Montreal), Jack Morris (signed as a free agent from Toronto), Charles Nagy, Mark Clark, and Chris Nabholz. While this rotation was certainly not going to be confused with the one the Indians had in 1954 that led to a then–American League–record 111 victories, it was still much better than Nagy, Jeff Mutis, Mesa, Mike Bielecki, and Clark starting in 1993. Martinez and Morris were the new veteran faces that had garnered much attention in the offseason, but Clark and Nabholz were young and unproven, and little was expected of them. Nagy was appropriately placed in the middle as the heart of—and key to—the Indians' pitching staff.

Selected by the club in the first round of the 1988 draft, Nagy had the potential to be the club's next homegrown mound stud after lefty Greg Swindell blossomed in the late 1980s. After pitching for the University of Connecticut and then for the 1988 U.S. Olympic Team (which won gold in Seoul, South Korea), Nagy first broke in with the Tribe late in 1990 before becoming a fulltime starter in 1991. Nagy put together a 4.13 ERA in 211⅓ innings but only managed a 10-15 record on the worst team (57-105) in Indians' history. The following year Nagy went 17-10 with a remarkable 2.96 ERA on a squad that improved its record by nineteen games. After leaving spring training in 1993 with a case of shingles and being put on the disabled list in mid-May with a shoulder injury that lasted the entire season, Nagy was now at the crossroads of his career. Would he return to be the kind of pitcher he'd been in 1992, or would he go down in the books as yet another opportunity missed for the Cleveland Indians?

Nagy had started answering those questions that Saturday when he went five solid innings against Pittsburgh, allowing just one earned run. And it only seemed appropriate that Nagy should start the first-ever (though not official) contest at the new ballpark. After all, he had started the final opening day game at Cleveland Stadium the previous April (and had been shelled in a 9-1 defeat to the Yankees without knowing he had shingles) and had come off the disabled list just in time to start the last game ever played at Cleveland Stadium (which he also lost, 4-0, to the Chicago White Sox.)

Despite how Nagy and the rest of the pitching staff performed, this team would be led by its offense, which suddenly had the potential to be one of the best in baseball. It appeared to be a balanced hybrid of youth and experience. General manager John Hart had complemented the signing of Martinez and Morris with the acquisition of veteran Eddie Murray to stabilize the lineup. With the proven triple threat of Kenny Lofton, Carlos Baerga, and Albert Belle anchoring the top portion, Hart had filled in the gaps with some other key moves. He traded shortstops with Seattle in December, picking up Omar Vizquel in exchange for Felix Fermin. Hart, manager Mike Hargrove, and the coaching staff kept young third baseman Jim Thome on the roster, along with once-shortstop-turned-utility infielder Mark Lewis and power-hitting first baseman Paul Sorrento. Veteran outfielder and designated hitter Candy Maldonado was in the middle of his second stint as an Indian and could fill in where needed with a dependable bat. Filling out the lineup was catcher Sandy Alomar Jr., who like Nagy was hoping to bounce back from injury to return to his award-winning form of 1990.

The toughest decision the Indians' brass had to make in Florida in March concerned who would start in right field: career minor-leaguer Wayne Kirby, who had broken in with the club in '93 and done a super job, or 1991 top draft pick Manny Ramirez, who would get the job in a matter of time regardless. Making the choice tougher, neither played his way out of competition in March. Kirby hit .352 with a pair of homers and fourteen RBI, while Ramirez went .370 with three home runs and eleven RBI. In the end the Indians decided to go with Ramirez as the starter and to keep Kirby on the roster as a backup who would see a lot of playing time before the end of the season.

Come what may, this team was ready to begin the season, and as the fans settled into their seats and gazed out at their new ballpark, the pregame entertainment began. At ten past noon, two groups of men wearing white dress shirts and slacks emerged from a section of fake cornstalks installed in the outfield in an obvious reference to the 1989 film *Field of Dreams*. The groups represented a pair of teams, one from Cleveland called the Forest Citys and one from Columbus called the Muffins, who took the field in an abbreviated game demonstrating the style of baseball in the mid–nineteenth century, including no bunting, no sliding, no balls and strikes, and, naturally, no swearing.

The old-time game was followed by a parade of old-time automobiles around the field on the rubberized track, including a 1936 Chevrolet in which Ohio Governor George Voinovich and Gateway executive director Tom Chema rode together in the rumble seat. The parade included the owners of the four retired jersey numbers in Indians' history: No. 19 (Bob Feller), No. 18 (Mel Harder), No. 5 (Lou Boudreau), and No. 3 (Earl Averill). Each member of the quartet was given a framed replica of his jersey just before his name and number were unveiled on the mezzanine level in right field in a reretirement ceremony. Then Voinovich, Chema, Cleveland Mayor Michael White, and Indians' owner Richard Jacobs each took turns in an elaborate ribbon-cutting ceremony at home plate.

In the meantime the president had arrived in the midst of the pregame festivities. Hart was giving Clinton a VIP tour of the new park, when suddenly the nation's commander-in-chief had to use the men's room. Luckily they were near the players' bathroom behind the Cleveland dugout, but when Clinton tried to open the door he discovered it was locked.

"Anybody in there?" the president asked. Both he and Hart heard a mumbled reply but couldn't comprehend it. A moment later the door opened, and there stood Indians' infield coach Buddy Bell, still zipping up his pants. By now nature was practically screaming at the president, and he didn't really notice Bell's awkward salutation. After the brief-but-vital pitstop, Clinton's tour continued.

Later, as the ceremonial first pitch drew closer, Clinton warmed up with Ryan Newman, the son of Indians' third-base coach, Jeff Newman. Though the president's daily schedule is usually chock full of places to be and people to meet, there was little doubt where he would be on opening day if the choice came down to which new ballpark to christen. The Ballpark at Arlington was the new crowning jewel of the Texas Rangers, owned by George W. Bush Jr., whose father Clinton had defeated in the 1992 presidential election. "It wasn't like [Bush] Junior was going to call him [Clinton]," said presidential aide James Carville. "I suspect the invitation got lost in the mail." Ironically, six years later, it would be Bush who received an invitation to replace Clinton as head of the American government.

The president then donned a new-style blue-and-red Indians' jacket and slapped on an Indians' cap. Trying not to offend any American Indian voters, Clinton chose a hat in the style the Indians had worn from 1978 to 1985, with a block letter "C" on it rather than the cartoon of Chief Wahoo, which the Indians had worn since 1986. Despite the president's selective choice of haberdashery, outside Jacobs Field a large group of protesters carried signs and handed out leaflets attacking the insensitivity of the Indians' mascot. Not far away another group was also exercising its right to free speech, protesting Clinton's new healthcare plan.

At 12:58, amid the Beatles' version of "Twist and Shout" playing over the loudspeakers, Clinton walked to the mound. Many figured that a man who had made thousands of speeches in front of millions of people during his political career would hardly break a sweat at lobbing a baseball fifty feet through the air to Sandy Alomar behind home plate in front of a measly 41,259 people. It was quite a different story.

"Actually, I was a little nervous," Clinton said in an interview for a video the team produced about the building of Jacobs's Field. "I was thinking I had just warmed up for fifteen minutes, but now I put on this big bulky baseball jacket and what if I blow it? What I did was take a deep breath, and I looked down there at Alomar and thought, 'He's a really big man! I can hit him! He's six-foot-six or something.'"

Once he started his delivery, Clinton admitted to not playing it exactly by the book.

"I cheated a little bit," he said. "I threw the ball a little higher and slower than I would if I were out there actually playing to make sure it got there without hitting the ground."

The ball did get to Alomar without bouncing, and a generous ovation gushed out of the stands. Voinovich followed Clinton with another first pitch, and Feller followed the governor with yet another.

The home plate these baseballs were sailing over had a connection to the Indians' past. It had been removed from Cleveland Stadium after the final game the previous October and inserted for this day to serve as a bridge in Indians' history. After the game, the plate would be replaced by a newer one and added to the team museum.

After fulfilling his presidential duties on the mound, Clinton walked around the field box area, high-fiving fans through the fence. Though it was a candid moment for the president, he was still surrounded by Secret Service agents who were watching his every move. "I could tell you how many (agents) are here," ballpark operations director Jim Folk told a reporter, "but I'd have to kill you afterward."

Finally, it was time for the starting lineups, introduced by new public address announcer Mark Tromba. The cards shaped up like this:

	Seattle		Cleveland
2B	Rich Amaral	CF	Kenny Lofton
3B	Edgar Martinez	SS	Omar Vizquel
CF	Ken Griffey Jr.	2B	Carlos Baerga
RF	Jay Buhner	LF	Albert Belle
LF	Eric Anthony	1B	Eddie Murray
1B	Tino Martinez	DH	Candy Maldonado
DH	Reggie Jefferson	C	Sandy Alomar Jr.
C	Dan Wilson	RF	Manny Ramirez
SS	Felix Fermin	3B	Mark Lewis

Fermin, the last Mariner introduced, received a warm ovation from the sellout crowd. Many remembered how long he had given his best effort as a member of some truly poor Indians' teams before the trade for Vizquel in December. "That made me feel good," Fermin said in the *Plain Dealer* of his reception. "I played here for five years and it's like a second home to me. When I was here, the fans were behind me 100 percent. Now that I'm with another team, they might be behind me forty percent."

The pitchers were also introduced: Randy Johnson for Seattle and Dennis Martinez for Cleveland. Ironically, the two had been teammates in Montreal in 1988 and 1989, when Johnson first broke into the major leagues. In four starts in

'88 Johnson made an immediate impression, winning three and compiling a
2.42 ERA in twenty-six innings. After seven uninspiring performances that resulted in four defeats early in 1989, Johnson was shipped to Seattle in late May
with relief pitcher Gene Harris in exchange for starting hurlers Mark Langston
and Mike Campbell. While the Expos had a reputation for losing whatever talent they did manage to develop, this would go down as one of the worst trades
in baseball history.

Johnson struggled to 7-9 his first year in Seattle but improved to 14-11 with a
3.65 ERA in 1990, his first full season in a Mariners' uniform. That summer he
showed an obvious indicator of what was to come when he tossed a no-hitter in
a 2-0 win over Detroit at the Kingdome on June 2. He slowly began blossoming
into one of the toughest pitchers in baseball over the next two seasons, and
despite collecting just a 25-24 record he consistently turned in ERAs under four.

At six-foot-ten, Johnson was the tallest man ever to play Major League Baseball, and his height combined with his blazing fastball worked to his advantage.
After leading the league in walks from 1990 through 1992, Johnson's control improved, and most hitters could count on getting strikes due to sheer intimidation
by the giant on the mound. In 1993 Johnson turned a corner, going 19-8 with a
3.24 ERA and a league-leading 308 strikeouts. Johnson had also enjoyed tremendous success against the Indians during his first five American League seasons,
holding a 7-3 record. He would now attempt to continue it in a new setting.

Martinez would also be looking for continued success while pitching his first
American League game in eight years. After breaking in with the Baltimore Orioles in 1976, the native Nicaraguan became a regular the following year when he
made forty-two appearances and compiled a 14-7 record. He started thirty-eight
games in 1978 and was a stalwart in the Orioles' pitching rotation in 1979, when
they won the American League pennant and faced the Pittsburgh Pirates in the
World Series. Martinez started Game Four and was shelled for four runs in less
than two innings, but Baltimore still pulled out the victory to take a commanding three-games-to-one lead in the series. Then the Pirates came back to win
three straight to take the title in Game Seven, and Martinez appeared in the
ninth inning of the seventh game.

He continued to be a key member on the Baltimore pitching staff through
the 1982 season, but the mental side of his game began affecting the physical.
Serious alcohol problems led to the start of Martinez's faltering with the Orioles
in 1983, a continuing downward spiral that hit rock bottom when he was sent
down to the minors during the 1986 season. With Baltimore (and future Cleveland) general manager Hank Peters wishing him a fresh start, Martinez was dealt

to Montreal on June 16, 1986, for infielder Rene Gonzales. It was exactly what Martinez needed, as his career made a dramatic U-turn in Canada.

Martinez went 11-4 in 1987 and then compiled a 2.72 ERA in 235⅓ innings in 1988. For the next five seasons Martinez was one of the most consistent pitchers in baseball, winning ten games or more in each season with an ERA never topping 3.85. His career hit a high point on July 28, 1991, at Dodger Stadium, when he pitched the sixth perfect game in National League history in a 2-0 win over Los Angeles. Two years later he became the seventh pitcher in baseball history to collect 100 wins in both the American and National leagues. After the season came to a close, the free-agent Martinez, who had spent eight seasons in Montreal and had never come close to a postseason appearance, signed with the Indians and was immediately the ace of the staff, despite being thirty-eight years old.

A small radio crew from Nicaragua would broadcast Martinez's Indians' debut back to his homeland, where he was so beloved that he'd been given the nickname "*El Presidente*," since many felt he could run for and win the nation's presidency. Though it would be one of twenty live radio and television crews broadcasting the game, it was the only one that hadn't brought any sophisticated equipment and wound up calling the play-by-play over the phone.

As Martinez prepared to take the mound, he took off his cap and held it over his heart while the Cleveland Orchestra and Chorus performed an inspiring version of "The Star-Spangled Banner." They drowned out the obnoxious buzz of a small plane floating overhead carrying an advertisement. As the anthem finished, hundreds of red, white, and blue balloons were released into the air from the outfield. A moment later home-plate umpire Larry Barnett, who had also called balls and strikes in the final game at Cleveland Stadium, stepped up to the microphone and bellowed the two words that fans of the game endure every long, dark winter for: "Play ball!"

Just before Martinez climbed the mound to toss the first pitch, Jacobs emerged from the Cleveland dugout to leave the playing field through an exit behind home plate. On his way he ran into Slider, the Indians' large, shaggy, purple mascot, dressed in a tuxedo for the occasion. The ball of fluff and the nearly eighty-year-old multimillionaire spontaneously began to dance, and for nearly ten seconds they provided probably the most memorable of all the pregame sights.

With the sun shining under clear blue skies and a forty-eight-degree temperature, Dennis Martinez toed the rubber on the pitcher's mound and prepared to make Cleveland sports history. A few hundred feet above, Tom Hamilton, the radio play-by-play voice of the Indians (along with the venerable Herb Score), set the stage:

Today this field of dreams has become a reality, and, boy, this reality has certainly exceeded everyone's expectations, he said. *What a beautiful ballpark and what a gorgeous Monday afternoon as Rich Amaral steps in. Dennis Martinez winds it up, and the season's first pitch . . .*

THE FIRST

	1	2	3	4	5	6	7	8	9			R	H	E
SEATTLE														
CLEVELAND														

April 4, 1994. The day three decades of losing and frustration floated off into the cool spring air. (*Akron Beacon Journal*)

. . . a called strike on the outside corner!

After receiving the ball, catcher Sandy Alomar tossed it to his left, where an Indians' employee caught it and raced it back into the dugout. It would eventually find a home in the team museum.

Rich Amaral hit Dennis Martinez's second pitch up the middle, but Carlos Baerga moved quickly to his right to field it and then made a smooth throw to Eddie Murray at first. The first batter of the season for the Seattle Mariners had grounded out—the first out in Jacobs Field history.

There's an old superstition in baseball that says that a team's fortunes for the season can be forecasted by the first at-bat of the year. Amaral's quick ground out may not have predicted the Mariners' future, but it certainly represented their past.

The Mariners first took the field almost exactly seventeen years earlier as an expansion team along with the first-year Toronto Blue Jays. Everything both teams did in the next decade-and-a-half served as a good case study in the history of the sport, since they were the first franchises born in the era of free agency in Major League Baseball.

In the champagne-soaked locker room at Yankee Stadium following the Cincinnati Reds' poetic sweep of the New York Yankees in the 1976 World Series, Reds' general manager Bob Howsam was asked what the future held for the Big Red Machine, with free agency set to begin in 1977. "We may never see what we had before," he replied. He had never been more right.

The Reds, like many of the dominant teams of the early 1970s, were dismantled and picked apart by free agency and would reach the playoffs just once in the next thirteen years. The term "dynasty" was thrown out of the baseball vernacular, as no team won back-to-back World Series between 1979 and 1992. Only the New York Yankees (1977–78 and 1998–2000)—a franchise that collects loads of extra revenue teams in smaller markets cannot, thanks largely in part to the fees paid for broadcasting rights—and the Blue Jays (1992–93)—when the Skydome was brand-new and sold out almost every night—won consecutive titles from the dawn of free agency through the end of the century.

This was the world the Seattle Mariners were born into on April 6, 1977, with a 7-0 loss to the California Angels.

The Mariners were actually Seattle's second major-league team in eight years. The Seattle Pilots were created in 1969 but lasted just one turbulent season. Because the Pilots managed to win just sixty-four games that year under manager Joe Schultz, poor attendance at the appropriately named Sicks Stadium cost the team's owners dearly. By the next spring they had little choice but to move the franchise. The Pilots reported to spring training in Arizona not knowing where they would be playing when the 1970 season began. Eventually the team headed to Milwaukee to become the Brewers four days before the regular season began, filling a void left in Wisconsin by the Braves when they moved to Atlanta in 1966. All of a sudden, Seattle had lost a baseball team as quickly as it had gained one. The league did promise the city another team in the next wave of expansion, which begat the Mariners and Blue Jays in '77.

The first edition of the Mariners' franchise was owned by six different people, including comedian Danny Kaye. But throughout the first decade of its existence, it was the players who provided most of the jokes. Seattle finished 64-98 in its first season, thirty-eight games behind Kansas City. It actually proved to be one of the more successful teams in the Mariners' first five years of existence, as they went on to lose 104 games in 1978 and 103 in 1980.

Now a city that had clamored for a baseball team throughout the 1970s was— justifiably—providing only half-hearted support. Only 22,588 attended the Mariners' 1980 home opener at the 59,000-seat Kingdome when pitcher Mike Parrott defeated Toronto. Serving as a symbol of the franchise's first four seasons, Parrott finished 1-16 that year with a paltry 7.28 ERA, while the Mariners came in last in the AL West once again. Manager Darrell Johnson was fired midseason and replaced by Major League Baseball's third black manager, Maury Wills, thus beginning a rapid-fire rotation of skippers in and out of Seattle throughout the 1980s. Wills was replaced midway through the "first season" of the strike-wrecked 1981 campaign by Rene Lachemann.

But 1981 had provided some long-overdue promise to Seattle fans. In January the team changed ownership, and a dramatic turnaround was promised. Early in the season outfielder Tom Paciorek cranked home runs in the bottom of the ninth inning in back-to-back games to defeat the eventual AL champion Yankees, and things finally appeared to be going the way of the Mariners. Paciorek went on to a career year in 1981, hitting .326, and the team did rally in the "second season" for a 23-29 record under Lachemann, 6½ games out of first place. What's more, the team had drafted pitchers Mike Moore and Mark Langston that summer, providing a future for the Mariners for the first time. As the 1982 season beckoned, Seattle didn't seem far off from contention.

The Mariners crept into fourth place that season with seventy-six victories, their best performance yet, but then tumbled back into the bowels of the American League in 1983 with their third 100-loss season. Making matters worse, the Blue Jays were now ready to contend and would make their first postseason appearance in 1985. Seattle seemed light years away from Toronto's success. Most of the Mariners' draft picks hadn't panned out, and they were unable to sign any big-time free agents to bolster their weak roster.

There were, however, some glimmers of hope. In 1984 Mark Langston went 17-10 with a 3.40 ERA, led the American League in strikeouts, and was named Rookie Pitcher of the Year by *The Sporting News*. That same season, first baseman Alvin Davis hit twenty-seven homers with 116 RBI and was the American League Rookie of the Year. Davis would prove to be one of the few models of consistency with the Mariners throughout the 1980s, although he never again matched the impressive power numbers of his rookie season. He stayed in Seattle through the 1991 season, after which he signed with California as a free agent.

Expectations were high going into 1985, as represented by the team's publicity slogan that season: "See It Happen." But all Mariner fans saw in the summer of '85 was more of the same, as Seattle matched its record from the year before and dropped to sixth place, seventeen games back of the world-champion Royals. Langston stumbled, but Mike Moore stepped up to win seventeen games. Chuck Cottier had replaced Del Crandall as manager during the 1984 season, and his modest success in 1985 earned him a new contract. But after a 9-19 start in 1986, Cottier was fired and replaced by Dick Williams.

The 1986 Mariners lost ninety-five games, and the hopes of a fruitful future in Seattle were once again looking bleak. One of the only bright spots of the season was the hitting of rookie Danny Tartabull. Mike Moore's record fell to 11-13, and Langston was still struggling to return to his rookie-season form, going just 12-14 despite once again leading the league in strikeouts. The Mariners *were* a part of history that season, but not in the way they had in mind. On April 29 at Fenway Park, Roger Clemens struck out twenty Seattle batters, setting a major-league record.

Before the 1987 season began, Tartabull and rising star Dave Henderson were traded away, and many expected another season of drudgery in the Kingdome. Seattle finished fourth, but this time they were only seven games behind the surprising world-champion Minnesota Twins at 78-84. Langston roared back into form with nineteen victories and again led the league in strikeouts. Manager Dick Williams wryly called it the greatest season in Mariners' history, and, unfortunately, it was. Through the Mariners' first eleven seasons, they still had not produced a winning record, but then it finally appeared they had turned a corner. After another lackluster start, Williams was dismissed the following June, and Jimmy Snyder directed the team for the remainder of the 1988 season. Once again the Mariners found themselves looking up at the rest of the American League West.

Jim Lefebvre took over in 1989, which as it happened, *would* be the season the Mariners started to turn the corner, although nobody knew it at the time. Their opening-day lineup featured a skinny nineteen-year-old kid by the name of Ken Griffey Jr., who would double in his first major-league at-bat and then hit home runs in his first two games in the Kingdome, setting the tone for a dazzling rookie season. Many felt Griffey's trip to the disabled list with a broken finger was the only thing that cost him the Rookie of the Year award. Seattle finished 73-89, twenty-six back of Oakland, but the Mariners had finally found a savior, and a new era of baseball was about to begin in Seattle.

During the belated spring training of 1990, following an owners' lockout, Athletics' manager Tony LaRussa said he thought five teams in the AL West were capable of winning the division, and he believed Seattle was one of them. The Mariners didn't win the division, but they did win seventy-seven games and finished fifth. The biggest story of the season was the uniting of Ken Griffey Sr. and Jr. in the Mariners' lineup. Griffey Sr. had been acquired after a short second stay in Cincinnati, and father and son teamed up to bolster the Seattle offense and bring positive national attention to the Mariners' dugout for the first time. Griffey Sr. hit .377 in seventy-seven at-bats in 1990, while his son hit .300 for the first time with twenty-two home runs and eighty RBI. Among the regulars, only third baseman Edgar Martinez overshadowed Junior's clip with a .302 average. With Griffey, Martinez, and young pitchers Erik Hanson and Randy Johnson beginning to show promise, what followed in 1991 only seemed natural.

Lefebvre left Seattle to take over the Cubs' managerial spot after the 1990 season, and Bill Plummer, once Johnny Bench's backup with the Reds, stepped in. The Mariners finally vaulted over the .500 mark in 1991 with an 83-79 record— nothing to throw a tickertape parade about, but for a team that had gone four-teen years without a winning season, eighty-three victories was nothing short of a miracle. What's more, the Mariners had only finished four games behind sec-ond-place Chicago and twelve back of Minnesota. Griffey had his first block-buster season, hitting .327 with twenty-two homers and 100 RBI. Edgar Martinez had his second straight .300 year, and Randy Johnson's ever-improving control earned him thirteen victories.

Although the nucleus seemed set, the success of 1991 was followed by yet another step backward in 1992, as Seattle lost ninety-eight games and finished last for the sixth time in sixteen years. Martinez had a career year, winning the American League batting title at .343, and Griffey kept pace with a .308 average but received little support from the rest of the team. Naturally, Plummer was removed as manager in the offseason.

His replacement was Lou Piniella, fresh off epic success and subsequent titanic disappointment as manager in Cincinnati. After managing the Yankees from 1986 to 1988, in 1990 he found himself taking over as skipper of the Reds after Pete Rose was banished from baseball. In his first year he led Cincinnati to a shocking sweep of Oakland in the World Series, but then struggled to a 74-88 mark in 1991. Although the team rebounded to win ninety games in 1992, the fiery Piniella was replaced by Tony Perez for 1993.

In Seattle, Piniella led the Mariners to their second winning season in 1993 at 82-80, good enough for fourth, eleven back of the Chicago White Sox. With the Mariners placed in the realigned American League West division in 1994, Piniella was expected to finally make contenders out of the Seattle Mariners.

He watched from the dugout as Amaral grounded out to open the season and Edgar Martinez stepped in for the Mariners' second at-bat.

Martinez had played in just forty-two games in 1993, shelved by a hamstring injury for most of the season. It broke a string of three consecutive .300 seasons that Martinez turned in from 1990 to 1992. He was hoping to get back to his old form as the 1994 season began on that sunny yet brisk afternoon in Cleveland.

He swung at and missed Dennis Martinez's 1-and-0 changeup and then fouled the third pitch deep down the right-field line and into Section 116 of the grandstand. There Rich Glinski, an interior decorator from Independence, Ohio, caught the first foul ball at Jacobs Field on the bounce, spilling his beer in the process. The sixth pitch in this battle of Martinezes was an 88-mph fastball that sailed inside and struck Edgar on the left wrist. The impact knocked his batting helmet off, and he fell to the ground. He got up slowly and jogged down to first, where he met the Mariners' trainer.

This was truly an inauspicious way to begin a season, especially after having missed three-quarters of the previous one with an injury. Edgar Martinez, the first baserunner in the history of Jacobs Field, stayed at first, and Ken Griffey Jr. stepped into the batter's box.

Griffey, a Cincinnati native, had been drafted by the Mariners at the age of seventeen in the first round of the 1987 amateur draft. In his first five years with Seattle, he had clobbered 132 home runs. But he wasn't just about offense. Shortly after his 1989 debut with the club, *Sports Illustrated*'s E. M. Swift compared his throws from the outfield to the cannon shots of Hall-of-Famer Roberto Clemente.

Griffey's father had enjoyed a wonderful career and won championships with the Big Red Machine in the 1970s. Conversely, Junior was now in his sixth major league season and had not come close to even contending for the playoffs. His hopes for the 1994 season seemed to epitomize those of the entire franchise.

He had hit .309 with forty-five homers in 1993, including a .449 clip against the Indians, with six home runs and twelve RBI in forty-nine at-bats. Now he was looking to do some early damage to Dennis Martinez in the first inning of the season.

The Cleveland outfield was shifted slightly right for the Seattle center fielder, who took the first two pitches for balls. Martinez's third pitch sailed high, and Griffey checked his swing on the fourth, which was just a shade off the plate. Griffey jogged to first, the beneficiary of the first walk in Jacobs Field history, and Edgar Martinez moved to second. The Mariners now had something going and only one out.

Jay Buhner stepped in as Seattle's cleanup hitter, coming off a 1993 season in which he had hit twenty-seven homers with ninety-eight RBI. The year before that, he was somewhat of a pioneer as he became the first right-handed batter to hit a home run over the right-center-field scoreboard at Camden Yards in Baltimore. Dennis Martinez would now try to keep him from placing any flags in yet-undiscovered territory at Jacobs Field.

Buhner fouled off Martinez's first pitch and took the second for ball one. After taking a pair outside and low, Buhner was up in the count 3-and-1, and Martinez was in danger of walking the bases full. He rallied with a perfect offspeed pitch that Buhner cut at and missed, but then Martinez missed outside with the payoff pitch. Buhner trotted down to first, sending Edgar Martinez to third and Griffey to second. The bases were now loaded for left fielder Eric Anthony, who had an opportunity to blast his way into the early annals of Jacobs Field lore.

Martinez's first pitch was a curve over the outside corner for strike one. Anthony clubbed the second offering to deep right field, but Manny Ramirez backpedaled to the ball and caught it four feet in front of the warning track for the second out. But Anthony's drive was deep enough for Edgar Martinez, who tagged and scored easily from third as Ramirez's throw was cut off at second. Griffey moved to third, and Buhner stayed at first. The Mariners led, 1-0.

Seattle first baseman Tino Martinez stepped in, hoping to improve in his third full season as a starter with the Mariners after hitting .265 with seventeen home runs and sixty RBI in 1993. The second Battle of Martinezes began as Tino watched Dennis's fastball sail right over the heart of the plate for strike one, then he crushed an offspeed pitch foul down the right-field line for strike two.

After another fastball sailed high and inside, Tino sent Dennis's fourth pitch, a curve, to shallow right field, where Ramirez called off Carlos Baerga to put it away and retire the side.

Dennis Martinez jogged back into the dugout, frustrated with himself. He had thrown twenty-four pitches in the first inning, twelve balls and twelve strikes, and had surrendered a run. He blamed the festive and lengthy pregame ceremonies for his lack of control early. "They told me the game was supposed to start at 1:05," he told the *Akron Beacon Journal.* "At 1:03 I was ready and set to go to the field. Someone came to the bullpen and told us they changed the time to 1:20, which might have had something to do with my wildness."

Though Jacobs Field was only a half-inning old, it was about to have its first historical presentation. As the Indians trotted off, a Cleveland grounds crew member removed first base and handed it to Eddie Murray, who had come back onto the field. This game, his first in a Cleveland uniform, marked the 2,369th he'd played at first, breaking the record set not by Lou Gehrig, as many supposed, but by Jake Beckley, who played with four teams from 1888 to 1907, including the Pittsburgh Alleghenies and the Cincinnati Red Stockings.

"You know, I have no idea who that person was," Murray said later. "He obviously had to have some stats, just to be out there that long. One day, I'd like to look him up in the books just to see all that he's done. I'm sure it's a lot." It was. Beckley had a .308 career batting average and collected 2,931 hits and 1,575 RBI.

Murray received first base and waved to the cheering crowd, then returned to the dugout. On further examination, the ceremony also seemed to point out how much more Eddie Murray had accomplished in his career than the Seattle Mariners had in theirs. Murray, who entered this game with 2,820 hits, ripped his first major-league safety the day after the Mariners first took the field in 1977. Since then Murray had won three Gold Gloves, been to two World Series, and played in eight All-Star Games. The Mariners' franchise could only aspire to one day accomplish as much as Murray.

In the first, the Mariners scored a run on no hits, and there were no errors.

	1	2	3	4	5	6	7	8	9		R	H	E
SEATTLE	1										1	0	0
CLEVELAND													

The Spin Doctors' "Jimmy Olsen's Blues" christened the Jacobs Field speakers as the first mid-inning song played in the park's history. It also served as a reminder that the Mariners' blues of the past seventeen years paled in comparison to those of the Cleveland Indians. Though the Indians existed for nearly eighty years before the Seattle Mariners took the field in 1977, from that moment to April 4, 1994, the franchises shared eerily similar fates.

Trying to embrace free agency right off the bat and turn around a franchise that had losing records in eight of the previous ten years, the Indians signed former Baltimore pitcher Wayne Garland to a ten-year, $2.3 million contract prior to the 1977 season. He had won twenty games for Earl Weaver's Orioles the year before, and the Indians' brass thought he was the marquee player who could push the club over the hump. It was a move that the financially strapped Indians couldn't afford to make, and it seemed to set the tone for the next fifteen years, especially when Garland injured his shoulder in his first exhibition game and went on to win just twenty-eight games for Cleveland over the next five seasons. By 1982 he was out of baseball, and the Indians once again seemed poised to leave Cleveland.

While the front office suffered a string of financial problems over the years, the Indians consistently fielded poor teams throughout the 1980s, including two 100-loss records in three years. Incidentally, they were the only team in the history of the game to sandwich a winning record (84-78 in 1986) between two 100-loss seasons (60-102 in 1985 and 61-101 in 1987).

Young prospects never seemed to pan out, while talented players never stuck around. The team was playing in ancient Cleveland Municipal Stadium, a terrible venue for baseball, and wasn't making any money off the puny crowds. Throughout most of the late 1970s and early 1980s the Indians were renting the Stadium from the Cleveland Browns and owner Art Modell, who took a good chunk of any profit the Indians collected. Cleveland had eight losing records in the 1980s and five different managers. It had never finished higher than fourth place in the American League East since the divisions were introduced in 1969, and before Jacobs Field was set to go, it appeared that there would be no end in sight.

But there were a few bright spots for the Tribe. On May 30, 1977, Cleveland pitcher Dennis Eckersley tossed a no-hitter against the California Angels. While this was certainly a great moment in Indians' history, it eventually became somewhat of a dark cloud over the team, reminding fans of what might have been. Less than a year later, Cleveland traded the talented young starter because his wife had fallen in love with his teammate Rick Manning. The Indians knew they had to trade one or the other, and they chose to trade Eckersley, figuring that with his awkward sidearm delivery, counting on his future success was somewhat of a gamble. Eckersley went on to have great success with Boston as a starter and then became one of the greatest closers of all time in Oakland, winning the AL Cy Young and MVP awards in 1992. Manning never hit higher than .263 with the Indians after the Eckersley deal and was traded to Milwaukee in June of 1983.

A possible savior appeared in 1980 with the arrival of center fielder Joe Charboneau, who hit .289 with twenty-three home runs and eighty-seven RBI on a promising 79-81 squad. Charboneau won the Rookie of the Year award, and it appeared that he would be a superstar mainstay in Cleveland throughout the 1980s. But he hit just .210 in forty-eight games with Cleveland the following year and spent most of 1981 in the minors. He appeared in just twenty-two games in 1982 before dropping off the face of baseball and into Cleveland's chambers of sports infamy.

On May 15, 1981, pitcher Len Barker threw the twelfth perfect game in baseball history, downing the Toronto Blue Jays, 3-0. After completing a sterling '81 campaign with a 3.92 ERA, Barker went on to have a solid 1982 season but was traded midway through 1983 for Brett Butler and Brook Jacoby. Barker retired after the 1987 season with a career record of 74-76.

The 1986 team was one of the best things to happen in Cleveland on summer nights since Ghoulardi went off the air. With a potent young lineup including Cory Snyder, Joe Carter, Brett Butler, Julio Franco, and Pat Tabler, along with dependable pitching from veterans like Tom Candiotti and Ken Schrom, the Tribe finished 11½ games behind pennant-winning Boston, and it appeared ready to roll. *Sports Illustrated* featured Snyder and Carter on the cover of its baseball preview issue the following April and predicted that the Indians would win the pennant. They didn't come close, losing 101 games as the franchise was once again dead in the water.

By 1988 most of the offensive talent from the '86 team was gone, but Cleveland's pitching staff had developed into one of the best in the business. The '88 squad set a team record with sixteen victories in the month of April and was just one game out of first in the second week of June before the expected slump set in. The Indians finished 78-84.

Over the next two seasons, starting pitchers Greg Swindell, Tom Candiotti, John Farrell, and Bud Black, along with closer Doug Jones, would help keep the Indians around .500 as the team waited for its ship to come in. Many thought the expensive free-agent signing of accomplished veteran first baseman Keith Hernandez prior to the 1990 season would be a part of the resurgence, but after hitting just .200 in forty-three games, the injury-riddled Hernandez retired.

Things looked brighter that spring when funding for the Gateway project was narrowly approved by Cuyahoga County voters. On the field, John McNamara was hired as manager, and fans hoped he could lead the team to that elusive next level just as he had done with Boston in 1986. And for the first time since Joe Charboneau ten years before, the Indians had a rookie of the year. This time it was catcher Sandy Alomar Jr., who hit .290 with nine home runs and sixty-six RBI in his first season in the Cleveland system since coming over in one of the greatest trades in franchise history.

On December 6, 1989, the Indians traded power-hitting outfielder Joe Carter to the San Diego Padres for Chris James, Carlos Baerga, and Alomar. Although fans criticized it at the time, as Terry Pluto would write five years later, it was the trade that broke what seemed to be a three-decade curse. With all three of the Carter-trade players contributing, the 1990 Indians finished the season on a roll and fueled high expectations for 1991.

Hopes quickly evaporated as the team got off to another terrible start, and McNamara was fired the first week of July. His replacement was coach Mike Hargrove, who did his best with the hand he was dealt over the last few months of the '91 campaign, but the Indians finished with the worst record in their history, 57-105. For much of that summer, no hope seemed to be in sight.

But as the bleakness of that season from hell neared its conclusion, there was a light at the end of the tunnel. After starting with the club as a scout, John Hart was tagged to replace Hank Peters as general manager. Peters had started the ball of progress rolling by pouring money into the farm system, something his predecessors never did. Hart then took the torch and introduced a new style of team management for the 1990s: he would sign his young players to longterm contracts *before* they became superstars to close down the revolving door that had become a tradition in Cleveland and help build a perennial winner. Hart planned the ultimate payoff to coincide with the opening of the new stadium in 1994. He initially started his plan by signing twelve young players, including Alomar, Baerga, Charles Nagy, and Steve Olin. A year later, Hart inked Albert Belle, Kenny Lofton, Paul Sorrento, and Felix Fermin to longterm deals.

The dividends were immediately seen in the second half of the 1992 season. After a typical 35-52 start, the Tribe finished the year on a 41-34 stretch that once more built up hopes for a promising future. Expectations were high in 1993, as the Indians hoped to contend in their final season at Cleveland Stadium before entering a whole new world at Jacobs Field the next summer. However, once again, things for the Tribe took a turn for the worse but not because of any poor decisions in the front office or lackluster performances on the field.

On March 22, two weeks before opening day, Cleveland pitchers Steve Olin and Tim Crews were killed in a boating accident in Florida during spring training, and fellow pitcher Bob Ojeda was seriously injured. Beyond the effect losing three talented pitchers had on the team, the players had to cope with the death of two of their teammates, and the game of baseball seemed trivial by comparison, even to the fans. Although the team managed to pull out its second straight 76-86 record, it was without question the most difficult season in Cleveland sports history. "You almost wipe everything off the slates from last year," ESPN's Chris Berman would say during the opening day broadcast from Jacobs Field. "Any mortal understands that."

It had, however, been a breakout season for the three players who would lead the team into a bold new future: center fielder Kenny Lofton, left fielder Albert Belle, and second baseman Carlos Baerga.

Lofton hit a dazzling .325 for the Indians in 1993, while Belle clobbered thirty-eight home runs (after hitting thirty-four the year before) and drove in 129 RBI. The switch-hitting Baerga had his second-straight .300 season at .321, with twenty-one home runs and 114 RBI. In 1992 he had become only the second second baseman in major-league history to hit .300, collect 200 hits, and get 100 RBI in one season. He did it again in 1993. The only other player to pull it off was Rogers Hornsby, who did it five times in the 1920s. It was clear that this trio would be the heart and soul of the Indians in 1994 and would ensure that the team would at least be decent. Anything beyond that would depend on what everyone else did.

And now, here on this beautiful April afternoon, were the new Indians, finally free of the albatross of the old stadium that had suffocated them for so many years. At last they were in a brand-new park to open a season full of expectations that this city hadn't seen on the baseball diamond in forty years. Appropriately, Lofton, the first of the three anchors of the Cleveland lineup, was also the initial Indian to bat at Jacobs Field.

Acquired from Houston along with Dave Rohde in a backpage trade in December of 1991 for pitcher Willie Blair and catcher Eddie Taubensee, Lofton made an immediate impact in 1992, his first full major-league season. Although he'd only played in twenty games in the big leagues before arriving in Cleveland, the speedy center fielder hit .285 and led the American League with sixty-six steals in 1992. He led the circuit again with seventy more in the following year. His speed and athleticism not only helped him out on the diamond but on the basketball court as well. In the late 1980s Lofton had to decide which sport he would pursue a career in: basketball, which he'd played at the University of Arizona (he was the sixth man on Lute Olsen's 1987–88 final-four team), or baseball. Lofton opted for baseball and was selected by the Astros in the seventeenth round of the '88 draft.

Randy Johnson, clad in his gray road uniform and his navy blue cap imprinted with an aqua "S" and a baseball and a navigational symbol crocheted in the middle, took his hat off and closed his eyes. He replaced his cap and crouched down, placing his glove on the ground and staring at it for a long moment. Then he rose, took the mound, and wound up for the first pitch of his season.

Though the unspoken rivalry between this pair wouldn't be truly manifested for another year, Johnson foreshadowed events to come with his first pitch of the season, a fastball that zipped inside and forced Lofton out of the batter's box. Possibly suffering from the same mental and physical setbacks as Dennis Martinez a few minutes before, plus a lengthy top of the inning, Johnson missed low on his next two pitches to Lofton and then walked him when his fourth hurl sailed inside. It was business as usual for Lofton as he trotted down to first, having drawn eighty-one walks in 1993, leading the team.

As Omar Vizquel's name was announced as he stepped into the batter's box, he received a polite—if not phlegmatic—response from the throng of Tribe fans. Little did they know what Vizquel would become to this franchise or what the trade that brought him here symbolized. More than any other move the Indians had made since the end of the '93 season, acquiring Vizquel best represented the turn the franchise was about to take.

Even more appropriately, Vizquel's first Cleveland at-bat would be against the team with which he had previously spent his entire career. Born in Caracas, Venezuela, Vizquel was signed as a free agent at the age of sixteen by the Seattle Mariners just before the 1984 season began. He broke onto the major-league roster in 1989, hitting .220 in 143 games. After spending half of the 1990 season in the minors and then an unremarkable 1991 campaign, Vizquel's career turned the corner in 1992. He led all American League shortstops with a .294 average, a sixty-four-point improvement from the year before. But more important, Vizquel had the best fielding percentage (.989) of all major-league shortstops, the seventh-best single season percentage in the history of the game. A year later he won his first Gold Glove, but his average dropped to .255, making him expendable in the eyes of the Mariners.

On December 20, 1993, the switch-hitting Vizquel was traded to the Indians in exchange for Reggie Jefferson and shortstop Felix Fermin, who up to 1994 had enjoyed a career almost identical to Vizquel's. Even on this opening day, many Cleveland fans didn't think much of the deal, but Seattle fans were already referring to December 20 as "Black Monday." In the years to come, Tribe fans would learn quite dramatically that their team had done more than simply swap light-hitting shortstops. Ironically, both Vizquel and Fermin started at shortstop in the same game, but they had traded uniforms since the previous year's opener.

Lofton bluffed a steal on Johnson's first delivery to the right-handed–batting Vizquel, and the pitch ran outside. Before making his second pitch, Johnson tossed over to Tino Martinez at first as Lofton dove back, his reputation preceding him. Still keeping an eye on Lofton, Johnson threw his second pitch high. After another bluff steal by Lofton on the third pitch, Johnson was down 3-and-0. Following seven straight balls, Johnson finally fired a strike with a blazing fastball down the middle, which Vizquel took.

On Johnson's fifth pitch, Lofton took off. Vizquel took another fastball strike as Seattle catcher Dan Wilson caught Johnson's pitch off the outside corner and fired it to second, where Fermin caught it perfectly situated in front of the base. He swept his glove and clearly tagged Lofton out a foot in front of the bag. Lofton knew he was outgunned and jogged back to the dugout muttering to himself.

But Wilson's putout was undermined a moment later when Johnson missed with his full-count pitch, and Vizquel trotted down to first, the recipient of Johnson's second straight walk. The second weapon in Cleveland's young triple-threat arsenal was now prepared to make his 1994 debut. Carlos Baerga climbed into the batter's box, also batting right-handed against the lanky southpaw.

Baerga had been the X-factor in the Joe Carter trade. Cleveland fans didn't know what to think at the time, but they came to understand the brilliance of the deal as the Puerto Rican quickly carved through the Indians' farm system. Baerga had been signed as an undrafted free agent by San Diego in 1985 but never saw any action at the major-league level until he debuted with the Indians in 1990. He appeared in 108 games that season, batting .260 with forty-seven RBI. Although his minor-league spot had been third base, Baerga won the starting position at second the following season and collected 171 hits while batting .288 on a 105-loss team. Along with Baerga's impressive hit totals and average during the '92 and '93 seasons, he also developed into a serious power threat in the three-hole to complement Albert Belle.

Johnson missed low with his first pitch to Baerga, the ninth ball of his first eleven pitches. Baerga hacked at one inside on the next toss and fouled it off. Vizquel took off on the third pitch and kept the Indians out of a double play as Baerga nubbed one off the end of the bat to Johnson, who turned, realized he couldn't get Vizquel, then tossed to Martinez at first to retire Baerga. Even though there were now two outs, the Indians would have their first opportunity to crack onto the new scoreboard with Vizquel in scoring position and their cleanup hitter, Albert Belle, stepping to the plate.

Drafted out of Louisiana State University by the Indians in 1987, Belle had already had a tumultuous career. Known as "Joey" during the early years of his professional career (short for his middle name Jojuan), Belle announced that he had an alcohol problem and entered a rehabilitation center after two brief and

ill-advised stints at the major-league level in 1989 and 1990. By the time his program was over, he was calling himself "Albert," and his career was about to take off.

He spent his first full year with the Indians in 1991 and hit .282 with twenty-
eight home runs and ninety-five RBI, but there were two incidents that seemed
to say more about him than any statistics could. First, Belle was sent down to the
minors as a punishment by manager John McNamara for not running out a
double play. Then, Belle drilled a fan in the chest with a baseball when the fan
taunted him from the outfield bleachers and called him "Joey." The incident—
which happened about the same time temperamental Cincinnati relief pitcher
Rob Dibble flung a baseball into the stands and hit a fan at Riverfront—earned
Belle another suspension. Despite all the controversy, his numbers went up in
1992 and 1993, and he was now on the cusp of becoming one of the premier
power hitters in all of baseball—if he could stay out of trouble.

He tried to hold up on Johnson's first pitch, a slider that twisted inside, but
went around for strike one. Vizquel started running on the second, which Belle
pounded into the ground toward third. Mike Blowers, filling in for Edgar
Martinez, who had left the game for precautionary X-rays of his wrist at Lutheran
Medical Center, fielded it and looked to his left, where Vizquel had stopped running six feet away. Blowers momentarily thought of trying to tag the Cleveland
shortstop, then thought better of it and fired across to Martinez. The delay seemed
to rush Blowers' throw, which flew off line, pulling Martinez off the bag. He
stretched out, caught it, and swept his glove around his side, swiping Belle across
the chest as he ran by with his arms in the air trying to avoid the tag. It was a
marvelous athletic move by Martinez, and along with catching Lofton at second, marked the second break of the inning for the Mariners.

In the first, the Indians scored no runs on no hits, and there were no errors.

THE SECOND

	1	2	3	4	5	6	7	8	9				R	H	E
SEATTLE	1												1	0	0
CLEVELAND	0												0	0	0

Call it League Park, call it Dunn Field, the Cleveland Indians called it home for nearly a half-century. (*Cleveland Press* Collection, Cleveland State University Library)

While the major players of the December trade between the Indians and Mariners had made their debuts in the first inning, the less noticeable player in the deal stepped up to lead off the top of the second.

Switch-hitting Reggie Jefferson held the designated-hitter spot for the Mariners on this opening day, as he had for the Indians in 1991 and 1992, although with limited success. Acquired by the Indians from Cincinnati in June 1991 for minor-league prospect Tim Costo, Jefferson had only played in fifty games over his first two seasons with the club and hit just .249 in 1993.

Batting left-handed, he cut at and missed Dennis Martinez's first pitch, serving as a quick demonstration that the thirty-eight-year-old pitcher knew he couldn't have another inning like the first one if the Indians wanted to send 41,459 people home happy on opening day. He nailed the outside corner on his second toss to go ahead 0-and-2, but then Jefferson showed that he was out to be a better hitter in 1994. He laid off a high curve for ball one, then fouled off the fourth pitch to stay alive. Then Martinez missed on three straight pitches: a curve that dipped low into the dirt, an offspeed pitch that sailed high, and another low curve on which Jefferson checked his swing, earning him a leadoff free pass to first base.

Dan Wilson stepped in and bunted the first pitch right back to the mound, where Martinez scooped it up with the intention to fire it to second to get Jefferson. But as he picked up the ball, he bobbled it momentarily and then wisely opted to get the sure out at first with Wilson. As he caught Martinez's toss, Eddie Murray nodded in agreement with his pitcher's decision.

With Jefferson at second and one out, Felix Fermin stepped in the box for his first at-bat since the final game at Cleveland Stadium the previous October. He smacked Martinez's first pitch to center, where Lofton moved a few steps to his right, caught the line drive, and quickly fired it back into the infield to keep Jefferson at second. Rich Amaral was up next.

Amaral took the first pitch of his second at-bat for a strike, then went ahead 2-and-1 when Martinez's next two tosses missed. Amaral spanked the third pitch foul past Mark Lewis down the third-base line, then ran the count full when a fastball sailed outside. Martinez's payoff pitch, a breaking ball, broke outside, and he had surrendered his fourth walk in less than two innings.

With two on and Griffey on deck, Martinez knew he couldn't fool around with Mike Blowers. He missed low with another breaking ball on his first pitch but came back first with a curve that Blowers swung at and missed, then with a fastball that nipped the outside corner. Blowers nubbed the fourth pitch down the first-base line, where Murray scooped it up and tagged the bag, ending the inning and getting Martinez out of trouble. Although his team only trailed by one, Martinez had thrown forty-two pitches in two innings—not a good sign for an aging veteran on a chilly day.

In the second, the Mariners scored no runs on no hits, and there were no errors.

	1	2	3	4	5	6	7	8	9		R	H	E
SEATTLE	1	0									1	0	0
CLEVELAND	0										0	0	0

Although it might have seemed like eons since the Indians had enjoyed a new toy box like Jacobs Field to keep their stuff in, 1994 was actually the third time a new major-league ballpark opened in Cleveland. The first came more than a century before.

At 4:08 P.M. on May 1, 1891, a twenty-four-year old pitcher from Gilmore, Ohio, named Deaton Young (nicknamed "Cy") fired the first-ever pitch at Cleveland's first true ballpark, which the *Plain Dealer* described as "the prettiest and best ball field in America."

"Deaton Young put a double reef in his trousers," the paper said of the first pitch, "wet a brand-new Spalding baseball with his fingers, smiled grimly, and then propelled his arm through space, releasing the ball as he did it."

The ball zipped past Bid McPhee and over the plate for a strike as the crowd roared its approval. The atmosphere was very similar on that day to that of another day nearly 103 years later, except that the Cleveland Spiders, not the Indians, were calling the new ballpark home, and the Cincinnati Red Legs, not the Seattle Mariners, were their opponents. But one thing these two opening days had in common was that they both marked the beginning of a new era of baseball in Cleveland and left a lot of history—*bad* history—behind them.

Cleveland's original professional baseball club, the Forest Citys, played their first game in July 1869 on a field called Case Commons located at what is now

East 38th Street between Scovill and Community College Avenues. The club used the Commons until it moved to the National Association Grounds, located at what is now Central Avenue and East 55th Street for the 1871 and 1872 seasons.

The original Forest Citys broke up following the '72 campaign, and Cleveland had no professional baseball until 1879, when a second club was established, this one called the Blues simply because of the color of their uniforms. The Blues joined the brand-new National League and played at National League Park, located at what is now Cedar Avenue and East 46th Street. But five years later Cleveland's team disbanded for the second time. After another edition of the Forest Citys lasted just the 1885 season in the Western League, the city of Cleveland was once again left without a team.

In 1887 a local businessman named Frank DeHaas Robison saw an opportunity to organize a new team and jumped at it. The latest edition of the Blues joined the American Association, a smaller organization comparable to the established National League. The team played at Brookside Park, located at what is now Payne Avenue and East 39th Street. When the name of the club was changed to the "Spiders" in 1889 (since there were so many tall and skinny players on the team), the name of their home field was also changed, appropriately, to Spider Park. That year also marked Cleveland's return to the National League.

A devastating thunderstorm in June 1890 caused considerable damage to Spider Park, and even though the team finished the season there, it was clear that a new home was needed. A new ballyard, originally called National League Park, after the home of the first Blues' club, was built at the corner of Lexington Avenue and Dunham Street, which, not coincidentally, was the hub for two streetcar lines owned by Robison and his brother.

There had been much speculation in the weeks leading up to the opening of the new park as to how many people would be in attendance for its first game. Most modest estimates said the crowd would number three or four thousand, while true optimists expected five or six. The Spiders hadn't helped encourage a big turnout with their recent play—they arrived back in Cleveland early on the morning of the opener after losing three straight in Pittsburgh, including a 4-3 defeat the day before. (Both the 1891 Spiders and 1994 Indians entered the first games in their new parks coming off defeats to the Pirates.) The optimists started to look pretty sage by midafternoon on May 1, as lines began forming at the ticket office at the corner of Beecher and Dunham by 2:30 P.M., ninety minutes before gametime under cool and overcast skies.

The Spiders arrived at 3 P.M. on a cable train as part of a sixteen-piece parade that swept through downtown and included a marching band and several circus animals. By then the ticket line was more than four hundred feet long, stretching all the way to Lexington. Meanwhile inside the park another marching band played for an hour leading up to the contest as the Spiders (wearing their white flannel uniforms with "Cleveland" sewn across the front in black letters) warmed up and chatted with the Red Legs (dressed, oddly, in blue flannels). All the while the crowd continued to grow, and the overflow stood in foul territory, roped off from the playing field.

By the time 4 P.M. rolled around, the stands were packed, and the dark coats and hats made up a solid ocean of black. Although there weren't many policemen on hand, the crowd did its best to keep out of trouble. Occasionally a bystander in search of a better view wandered out onto the field and got in the way of the players, but no real problems arose. In all, more than nine thousand people settled in to watch the Spiders and Red Legs go to battle. Getting the huge crowd into the park only created a slight delay, and the first pitch was stalled a few moments longer when a photographer standing in center field took a few extra moments to snap a picture.

After holding Cincinnati scoreless in the opening frame, the Spiders came to bat for the first time ever at League Park. Youngstown native Jimmy McAleer ripped a shot into the gap in right center for the game's first hit and reached second easily. However, with the roar of the mammoth crowd, he couldn't hear his third-base coach advising him to stay there, and he was thrown out at third. It would be one of the few sour points in an otherwise sweet day for Cleveland. The Spiders broke onto the scoreboard a few moments later, following a George Davis walk and a Cupid Childs RBI double. Ralph Johnson followed with a single up the middle that drove in Childs to give the Spiders a 2-0 lead. It would almost be enough for Young, who was magnificent on this day. No Cincinnati batter got past first base during the first seven innings, while the Spiders added another run in the fourth.

Just before Cleveland batted in the bottom of the fifth, three wild geese flew over League Park, honking. Someone in the crowd yelled, "That means three runs!" And sure enough, the Spiders scored three times in the fifth, making the score 6-0. With Young pitching, it was all over but the shouting. Cleveland added a pair in the sixth, and when the Red Legs plated three in the top of the eighth, the Spiders bounced back with four of their own to win going away.

By the time the dust settled a mere hour and fifty-eight minutes after the game had begun, Cleveland had broken in its new park with style. The Spiders collected their fifth straight win over Cincinnati with a 12-3 stomping that put them in a tie for first place in the National League with the Boston Beaneaters.

"It was a great game for a home audience to see, but Cleveland won it so easily that there wasn't much cause for any legitimate and constant excitement," declared the *Plain Dealer*. "The home team gave a magnificent exhibition of fielding, base running and hitting—especially hitting."

Cleveland shortstop Ed McKean and first baseman Jake Virtue had collected three hits apiece, and two of Virtue's safeties were triples. The second of his three-baggers, which came in the eighth, was the longest hit ball of the day, even longer than Arlie Latham's home run for Cincinnati in the seventh. Cleveland second baseman Childs also drove in four runs.

Just as many Clevelanders argued in the early 1990s that the Indians were so bad they didn't deserve a new stadium, the same contention was made a hundred years earlier with the Spiders. After racking up a downright offensive 89-174 record in the American Association during the 1887 and 1888 seasons, the Spiders went 61-72 in their first National League season in 1889. They were even worse in 1890, dropping to 44-88, but the opening of League Park resulted in the first baseball renaissance in Northeast Ohio. The Spiders improved to 65-74 in 1891 and then catapulted to 93-56 under manager Oliver "Patsy" Tebeau the following year. It was the first of seven consecutive winning seasons for the Spiders, although they never finished first in the National League.

In 1895 the Spiders went 84-46 and finished second to the Baltimore Orioles, who were led by a feisty third baseman named John McGraw. The two teams squared off in a championship series called the Temple Cup, sparked by the interest of a wealthy Pittsburgh native named William H. Temple, who wanted to see postseason baseball between the league's first- and second-place finishers. He donated a large silver cup that would go to the best-of-seven champion along with the majority of the ticket proceeds. The Orioles had nonchalantly been swept in four games by the second-place New York Giants in the first Temple Cup in 1894.

The 1895 series turned out to be a cavalcade of rowdy behavior. Both the Orioles and the Spiders had earned reputations as wild and dirty teams, and while the Temple Cup didn't seem to bring out the worst in them, it certainly evoked it from their followers. Fans at League Park pelted, amongst other things, vegetables, seat cushions, and beer bottles at the Orioles, then Baltimore fans returned the favor in Maryland, assaulting the Spiders' horse-drawn carriage with rocks and bricks. The Spiders took the Cup in five games and won a total of $580 from the gate.

Baltimore and Cleveland met again the following year in the Temple Cup as the Spiders tried to avenge another second-place finish in the postseason. They had no such luck this time, as the Orioles swept them in four games and captured their second Temple Cup. But fan interest had waned throughout the 1896 season, and the Baltimore club received just a $200 winners' share from the championship series. The Spiders slipped to fifth in 1897, and the Orioles won their second and final Temple Cup. The series was eliminated that autumn as an anticlimax to the pennant race and wasn't making much money. After maintaining the status quo in the 1898 standings, the Spiders' string of successes, initiated with the opening of League Park, finally ran out.

In 1899 Robison bought a controlling interest in another National League club, the St. Louis Browns. Robison believed there was more money to be made in St. Louis than Cleveland and began moving all of the talented Spiders to the Browns, including manager Tebeau and superstar Cy Young. Naturally the result was Cleveland having arguably the most embarrassing professional baseball team ever. The Spiders compiled the worst won-loss record in major-league history at 20-134, a whopping eighty-four games behind the first-place Brooklyn Superbas. Things were so bad that midway through the season Robison closed up League Park and had the Spiders play all their remaining home games on the road.

Not surprisingly, the following year Robison sold the team to John Kilfoyl and Charles Somers and focused his attention on the St. Louis Browns. Meanwhile a former sports editor from Cincinnati named Ban Johnson set out to form an association to compete with the twenty-four-year old National League. Johnson swept together what he could from the shattered remains of the old American Association and a minor-league circuit he'd operated called the Western League. He also brushed Cleveland into his dustpan, then shook it all out to form the American League. After one year of minor-league status in 1900, which included a Cleveland team called the Lake Shores, the American League began play as a rival major league in 1901.

Longtime Spiders' fans may have felt jilted about the method of their team's demise, but could take heart in the fact that Robison's St. Louis teams never competed for the pennant. The greedy owner got a taste of his own medicine when several of his players (as well as many other National Leaguers who felt abused by their owners) left the senior circuit to join the newly formed American League. When Cy Young left St. Louis to join the Boston Somersets in the AL, he told Robison, "Your treatment of your players has been so inconsiderate that no self-respecting man would want to work for you if he could do anything else in the world."

The Spiders were replaced by the Lake Shores, who begot the Bluebirds, Cleveland's first entry in the American League. They became the Cleveland

Bronchos, then the Cleveland Naps. After popular player-manager, future hall-of-famer, and team namesake Napoleon Lajoie stepped down as manager in 1909, the Naps became the Cleveland Indians. Over the years the official legend stated that fans chose the new name through a contest in a local newspaper. "Indians" was reportedly suggested by a fan to honor the first American Indian to play professional baseball, Louis Sockalexis, who played with the Spiders from 1897 to 1899.(Further investigation reveals otherwise. In his 1999 book *Our Tribe*, Terry Pluto suggests that team officials selected "Indians" in homage to the Boston Braves of 1914, who had rallied to win the world title after being in last place in early July. The Sockalexis connection was more of a happy coincidence.)

All of these Cleveland teams called League Park home. For a while the Indians hung their hats at "Dunn Field," as new owner James Dunn brashly renamed the park after himself in 1920. Dunn died in 1922, and his estate sold the team to Alva Bradley in November 1927. Bradley reverted the name back to League Park. The new field would be used on a daily basis for forty-one seasons, and although it was renovated along the way (the most significant renovation taking place after the 1910 season when capacity was increased from 9,000 to 21,000), it eventually became the smallest stadium in the American League.

In some ways Jacobs Field was built almost in homage to League Park. While the Jake's left-field wall stood nineteen feet high and a brief 325 feet from home plate, League Park's right-field fence stood forty feet tall and was a mere 290 feet out. The architects of Jacobs Field put in the mini–Green Monster as a novelty to evoke memories of the ballparks of yesteryear, but the right-field giant at League Park was built out of necessity. The owners of a saloon and two houses in the neighborhood outside the park refused to sell their properties to Robison when he was buying up land for the construction. Therefore League Park, like the Polo Grounds in New York, had a ridiculously long center field (varying between 450 and 467 feet through the years), an average left field, and the oddity of right. Plus, for big games with overflow crowds like the 1891 opener, seating was extended into right field and roped off, shortening the distance to 240 feet.

Many of the walls at League Park were made of concrete with metal screening covering other portions, but the towering right-field wall included steel beams, which would create quite a spectacle when balls hit them, and outfielders were forced to chase after odd hops.

With left field bordering East 70th Street, the third-base line traveling along Linwood Avenue, the first-base lane parallel with Dunham Street (eventually renamed East 66th Street), and Lexington Avenue just outside of right field, League Park was very much a part of the neighborhood, much like Jacobs Field would be a century later. If a ball did clear one of the fences and escape into the streets around League Park, children could bring it back to the park and receive free admission.

In 1994 Indians' fans were hoping Jacobs Field would soon be the site of a World Series. Cleveland fans had to wait seventeen years after the Fall Classic began for it to come to League Park, but it was well worth the wait. The 1920 Indians defeated the Brooklyn Dodgers five games to two to capture Cleveland's first baseball championship since the 1895 Temple Cup. It was a series that saw the first-ever unassisted triple play (by Cleveland's Bill Wambsganns) and the first-ever grand slam (by Cleveland's Elmer Smith) in World Series history, both at League Park, in a 8-1 Indians' win in Game Five.

By the time Jacobs Field was completed, League Park had long since been demolished, purchased by the city of Cleveland and turned into a public park in 1951. League Park's legacy holds strong in Cleveland athletic lore even to this day, and no one who saw a game there will ever forget it. It was the first legitimate home for the city's baseball team, and it began a new chapter in civic athletic history.

On that first opening day in 1891, the *Plain Dealer* probably put it best: "There never was one like it and there may never be another," the article said. "Baseball is very much alive in Cleveland."

That statement could also apply to the situation 103 years later, as Cleveland baseball fans of 1994 welcomed a much-needed veteran boost to their club's lineup when Eddie Murray stepped to the plate.

There wasn't much Murray hadn't done in his seventeen-year career. After breaking in with the Baltimore Orioles as American League Rookie of the Year in 1977, he quickly became one of the best players in the game. Two years later, he helped the Orioles reach the World Series by batting .417 in the American League Championship Series against California. After a New York sportswriter composed a story full of inaccuracies about Murray's family, Murray struggled severely in Baltimore's seven-game loss to the Pittsburgh Pirates. Although it may have just been coincidence, from that point on he was always very cautious with his words and rarely spoke to the media.

In his fourth major-league season Murray hit .300 with thirty-two homers and 116 RBI. He hit sixty-five home runs total in 1982 and 1983 and batted over .300 in each season, the latter of which ended with the Orioles defeating the Philadelphia Phillies in the World Series. Murray became one of the most consistent players in baseball and the man to whom young Oriole Cal Ripken Jr. attributed his philosophy of giving all you had every day. After the 1988 season Murray was traded to Los Angeles, where he had grown up. He left Baltimore as the team's all-time home-run leader and was second in hits and RBI. After a sub-par 1989 Murray exploded in 1990 by hitting a career-high .330. Following another solid season in 1991 Murray signed with the New York Mets as a free agent and spent a pair of tumultuous seasons with one of the worst teams in the worst media city in baseball. "My two years there felt like five," Murray said to Pluto in 1995. "In New York, the media doesn't want you to do well. I don't know if the media in Cleveland could act like the guys in New York, even if they wanted to."

At the end of his contract Murray wanted to be anywhere but New York. Meanwhile John Hart was looking for someone to bat fifth in the Cleveland lineup behind Albert Belle to ensure that he'd see good pitches. Paul Sorrento didn't exactly strike fear in the hearts of American League pitchers the way that someone like an Eddie Murray would. At the same time Murray was looking for the antithesis of New York and everything it represented. It was a match made in heaven.

Not coincidentally, Murray and Dennis Martinez both signed with the Indians on December 2, 1993. And by the time this opening day was over, they would both have made immediate impacts on this team as the quintessential veterans they were.

Fans didn't get a chance to enjoy Eddie Murray's first plate appearance as an Indian very long. He powered Randy Johnson's initial pitch into right field, where Jay Buhner ran to his right, turned around as the wind altered the ball's flight path, and caught it three feet in front of the warning track for the first out.

While Murray may have been an icon for the sport in the 1980s, if one were to look up the word "journeyman" in the dictionary of baseball, he'd probably find a picture of the next Indian to bat, Candy Maldonado. After cracking into the show with Los Angeles in 1981, he spent five mediocre seasons with the Dodgers before moving on to San Francisco, where he had the best year of his career in 1987, hitting .292 in 118 games while helping the Giants win the NL West. He was picked up as a free agent by the Indians in 1990 and became the team's only true power hitter, despite having just twenty-two home runs and ninety-five RBI. He played with the Milwaukee Brewers and Toronto in 1991 and earned his place in baseball history books the following October. As a member of the Blue Jays in Game Three of the World Series against the Atlanta Braves, Maldonado hit a bases-loaded single that drove in the winning run in the ninth inning, giving Toronto a 3-2 win and a two-games-to-one advantage in the series. The Blue Jays would go on to win, four games to two. After spending half of the 1993 season as a Cub, Maldonado returned to Cleveland where he hit .247 in twenty-eight games.

Facing Randy Johnson on opening day 1994 Maldonado was part of a team that badly needed any experience he could provide. He took Johnson's first offering, a fastball low, then took another fastball at the knees for strike one. After a third-pitch slider hit the dirt for ball two, Maldonado slapped a fastball sharply to the right side, where Amaral made a diving stop to his left at the edge of the grass. He threw to first from his knees for the second out, bringing up Sandy Alomar Jr.

If there was one man who deserved to be on a winning baseball team in Cleveland, it was Sandy Alomar. After being named American League Rookie of the Year four years earlier, Alomar had faced enough adversity to last a career. He only played in fifty-one games in 1991 because of suffering injuries to his shoulder and hip. Then he missed nearly half of 1992 with torn webbing between his fingers and torn cartilage in his knee. In limited action Alomar hit just .238 in those two years. Still he became the first Indian elected by the fans to start in three consecutive All-Star Games, more a tribute to the wonders of sports marketing than to his onfield performance. The 1993 season was more of the same, and Alomar appeared in just sixty-four games due to a ruptured disc in his back.

Many fans had forgotten how good Alomar was when he wasn't injured. They had forgotten how he threw out runners from his knees as a rookie or how he could smother a wild pitch like a brush fire. Possibly adding to Alomar's frustration was the success of his younger brother, Roberto, who had just won back-to-back world championships with Toronto in 1992 and 1993. The pair had played together briefly with the San Diego Padres in 1989 before Sandy was shipped to Cleveland and Roberto to Toronto a year later. In the years to come they'd often wonder what it would be like to play on the same team again, once both were established as stars of the game.

But now Sandy Alomar wasn't thinking about a reunion with his brother; he was concentrating on reaching base. Going into the at-bat 0-for-9 in his career against Randy Johnson, Alomar fell behind 0-and-2 as he was fooled first by a fastball and then a curve. After fouling an outside pitch down the right-field line, Alomar evened the count by laying off a pair of outside pitches. He fouled off Johnson's sixth pitch into the right-field seats, then tapped a soft grounder off the handle of his bat to Amaral at second, who threw him out.

Make that 0-for-10.

In the second, the Indians scored no runs on no hits, and there were no errors.

THE THIRD

	1	2	3	4	5	6	7	8	9		R	H	E
SEATTLE	1	0									1	0	0
CLEVELAND	0	0									0	0	0

Resting like an iron giant on the shores of Lake Erie, Cleveland Municipal Stadium personified the inadequacies of the Indians for more than sixty years. (*Cleveland Press* Collection, Cleveland State University Library)

It only seems fair that the man who was issued the first-ever walk at Jacobs Field should also be the victim of the ballpark's first-ever strikeout.

Ken Griffey Jr. fouled back Dennis Martinez's first offering, an offspeed pitch, to lead off the third, then took a curve at the knees for strike two. After taking a fastball that just missed inside, Griffey was fooled by the crafty Martinez, who came back with the exact same pitch. Expecting something outside, Griffey waved weakly at the ball, trying to foul it off. He missed and returned to the dugout, forever carving his name in Jacobs Field lore as the first official whiff at the new yard.

Jay Buhner stepped in next and took Martinez's first two offerings, both curveballs—one high for a ball and one at the letters for a strike. He fouled the third pitch down the third-base line and then tapped the fourth off the end of the bat to Omar Vizquel, who threw him out. It was the first putout by Vizquel in a Cleveland uniform.

Another exhibit to the case for proving that baseball is a funny game, Eric Anthony made his second at-bat of the season even more memorable than his first. Anthony, who had never collected more than eighty RBI in his first five seasons in the majors, had picked up the first-ever at Jacobs Field with a sacrifice fly in the first. Now, after taking a breaking ball low and inside, he was about to ring up his second in as many at-bats.

Martinez fired a fastball that drifted too far out over the plate right at the letters, and Anthony belted it toward right. Manny Ramirez gave chase but stopped as the ball just cleared the fence and landed in the Seattle bullpen. The 352-foot shot, which never reached more than fifteen feet off the ground, put the Mariners ahead 2-0 and made Anthony an opening-day candidate for American League MVP. Although no one realized the significance of this at the time, it was appropriate that the first hit at Jacobs Field was a home run.

Dennis Martinez came back with a first-pitch curveball strike at the knees to Tino Martinez, then missed with a breaking ball in the dirt to even the count. Tino Martinez pounded the 1-and-1 pitch to Murray at first base, who jogged to the bag for the third out. It would be one of Dennis Martinez's quickest innings of the day, but it also dug the Indians into a deeper hole.

While the Mariners' future looked bright midway through the third on this opening day, a reminder of past failures and missed opportunities came from 650 miles away. At Fenway Park in Boston, former Mariner Mike Moore had just surrendered a home run to Andre Dawson, as the Tigers fell behind the Red Sox. Although it was a sour moment for Moore, the fact that he was Detroit's opening-day starter proved that he was an asset Seattle could have used in 1994.

In the third, the Mariners scored one run on one hit, and there were no errors.

	1	2	3	4	5	6	7	8	9			R	H	E
SEATTLE	1	0	1									2	1	0
CLEVELAND	0	0										0	0	0

No one who attended the opening of League Park was around to take in the inaugural festivities at Jacobs Field, but a few people could still recall the last time the Indians threw a housewarming party.

"Do I remember it?" former Cleveland pitcher Mel Harder once said, as quoted in Russell Schneider's *Cleveland Indians Encyclopedia.* "How could I ever forget? Pitching that game was the biggest thrill of my career."

Harder wasn't talking about an opening-day celebration, however. On the last day of July 1932 the Indians hosted the defending American League Champion Philadelphia Athletics in a game that would prove to not mean much in the final standings. The Indians were destined for a fourth-place finish under manager Roger Peckinpaugh, while the Athletics would come in a distant thirteen games behind the pennant-winning Yankees. It was nothing more than a midsummer matchup between two also-rans in the record books, except, that is, for the location of the contest. The teams played in the first-ever baseball game at brand-new Cleveland Municipal Stadium before a packed house, with nearly twice as many spectators as would be at Jacobs Field sixty-two years later.

Despite their considerable differences in size, the origins of Cleveland Stadium and Jacobs Field are strikingly similar.

The concept of a lakefront stadium downtown began in the mid-1920s as a small venue—not much bigger than League Park—that could be used for minor events such as high school football. The idea grew (both literally and figuratively) in the following years, and in 1926 city manager William Hopkins asked

Osborn Engineering Company to design a preliminary model for a huge ballpark, one that could seat between 80,000 and 100,000.

Hopkins met with then–Indians' president Ernest S. Barnhard to discuss the possibility of the new stadium. Although Barnhard liked the idea of more available seats to sell, he was originally uncomfortable with the idea of having his team play in a stadium owned by the city. At the time, every Major League Baseball team owned the park it played in. (Certainly over the next sixty years that thinking would change dramatically.)

After Barnhard departed Cleveland to become the commissioner of the American League, new Indians' owner Alva Bradley supported the idea of a new park, though he wasn't terribly concerned about whether or not the citizens would be willing to pay for it. If the city wouldn't build the stadium, he thought, the team would just lease the land and pay for it itself. City officials smelled the money that Cleveland could potentially rake in from a huge stadium and sprang to action. In August 1928 the city council authorized a $2.5 million bond issue to be placed on the November ballot to pay for the new stadium, which, proponents boasted, could be used for more than sixty different kinds of activities, ranging from baseball to operas. In later years an urban legend was conceived that city officials hoped to draw the 1932 Summer Olympics to Cleveland. This was never publicly discussed, although those in favor of the new stadium believed that that was the kind of versatility the project could bring. More than just a venue for sporting events, many saw the stadium as a springboard that would catapult Cleveland into the upper echelon of American metropolises. No city could be considered a big city without a major stadium.

Thus, unlike Jacobs Field, the bond issue passed comfortably by a margin of 59 percent to 41 percent (112,448 votes to 76,975). It would be the first new stadium featuring metal construction elements and, more notably, would be the first-ever municipally owned ballpark. "The Stadium will be an enduring monument to the spirit and aspirations of our people," said city manager Daniel Morgan, who replaced Hopkins in 1930. The architectural firm of Walker and Weeks was tapped to design it.

But as the landfills along the lake were prepared for construction, the project hit some legal snags. Opponents filed motions and argued any way they could to keep the stadium from being built. In May 1929 a citizen named Andrew Meyer filed a taxpayer suit in Cuyahoga County Common Pleas Court to stop construction. He cited several issues, some technical concerning the city council's wording of ordinances. Most notably he said, 1) that the funds the city asked for would be inadequate to pay for the entire project, and 2) that since the stadium would most benefit the Indians, a private business, it would fail to serve a legitimate public purpose. (Meyer may not have garnered much support at the time, but clearly his thinking was ahead of his time.) City lawyers spent a year fighting the suit, winning at the common pleas and district levels, but it wasn't until the Ohio Supreme Court decided not to hear the case that construction could begin.

The groundbreaking took place on June 25, 1930, sixty-two years to the day before Charles Nagy and Mel Harder threw the ceremonial first pitches at the Jacobs Field site. Official construction began on July 28 by the Osborn Engineering Company, which had also worked on Yankee Stadium, Fenway Park, and Comiskey Park. Not long into the construction, planners realized that Meyer had been correct, at least about the funding. They were forced to cut corners and change plans in order to slice the budget back to its $2.5 million price tag. Still, thanks mostly to the mildest winter in recent memory, construction hummed along.

But an even darker cloud loomed over the creation of Cleveland Stadium when, on January 30, 1931, high winds snapped the cables holding a scaffolding tower in place, and it collapsed, plummeting a pair of ironworkers 120 feet to their deaths. "Although there were times when more than 2,000 men were employed at one time in construction of the Municipal Stadium, only two fatalities marred the completion of the structure," callously reported the *Plain Dealer* upon the stadium's opening.

Despite the setbacks the project was completed on July 1, 1931, in a mere 370 days. It's interesting that despite the dramatic growth in construction technology, Jacobs Field took nearly twice as long to build sixty years later.

Cleveland Stadium officially opened with a formal dedication on July 2. City officials anticipated a huge crowd, maybe better than 75,000. To their surprise a mere 8,000 turned out. This theme would last throughout the stadium's existence. It popped up again the following night at the stadium's first athletic event, a title bout between Max Schmeling and Young Stribling. Stadium officials considered the possibility of a crowd better than 100,000. Instead, it was a modest 37,000.

Although the magnificent new stadium was now completed, there was one problem. The city did not ink a formal agreement with the Indians for use of Cleveland Stadium during its construction, and as it opened the city and team could not agree to terms. A year would pass before the Indians played their first game at the "new" ballpark. What's more, as Andrew Meyer had predicted, the final cost of the stadium was about a half-million dollars more than what had appeared on the ballot in 1928. This overflow was because of the last-minute addition of lights (which wouldn't be used for an Indians' game for eight years), an

electronic scoreboard, and a sound system, in addition to the construction of au-
tomobile and pedestrian bridges to the stadium over the lakefront railroad tracks.

Despite the cornucopia of problems Cleveland Stadium presented, all was
forgotten on the sunny Sunday afternoon of July 31, 1932. The impressive mammoth resting like an iron giant on the shores of Lake Erie didn't look like anything that could have been conceived during a depression that had crippled the
nation. It was, for that day at least, the mighty symbol of prosperity that
Clevelanders had longed for. And just as with the opening of League Park forty-
one years before and with the opening of Jacobs Field sixty-two years afterward,
the first game at Cleveland Stadium created quite a bit of hoopla and featured
six future hall-of-famers in the starting lineup.

Fans from all over the state made their way to the North Coast to see this new
wonder. Cleveland Stadium made a record-breaking debut, setting the single-
game major-league attendance mark. "I'm mighty glad to be here myself," Governor George White told the *Plain Dealer,* "and I'm glad to see that half of Ohio
is here, too."

With 76,979 in paid attendance, 3,005 in on passes, and 200 employees, a
grand total of 80,184 were on hand for the ballgame, a crowd that would have
formed the ninth-largest city in the state of Ohio. The previous attendance record
was set on September 9, 1928, for a doubleheader at Yankee Stadium, when 80,043
saw the Athletics go to battle with the Yanks.

The Goodyear Blimp floated over the scene as the ocean of spectators flooded
into the new ballpark and the pregame festivities began. Baseball comedians
Nick Altrock and Al Schacht entertained the crowd before the game, then several of the great names in Indians' history, who had been invited to christen the
new yard, were introduced. Included were Paddy Livingston, Elmer Flick, Earl
Moore, former manager Lee Fohl, Bill Wambsganss, Elmer Smith, Cy Young,
and Tris Speaker—a man public-address announcer Jack Graney called "the
greatest center fielder in baseball history."

A few moments later Graney simply cried, "Larry Lajoie!" The crowd responded in unison, "Larry Lajoie!" Then Napoleon "Larry" Lajoie, who had
played for the club from 1902 to 1914 and managed them between 1905 and 1909,
waltzed onto the field to a hearty round of applause. Graney next introduced "a
man who does as much for baseball as any living man," and Philadelphia manager Connie Mack stepped out of the dugout to a thunderous ovation.

Another living piece of history was on hand for the event, but not just as a
dignitary or spectator. Home plate umpire Tom Connolly was chief of umpires

for the American League and had officiated at the grand openings of five other new ballparks. Connolly had been on the field for the first games at League Park, Fenway Park, Comiskey Park, Yankee Stadium, and Griffith Stadium in Washington, D.C. When asked what he thought of Cleveland's yard, Connolly replied, "Fine, only I wish they had hooks in the umpires' room," foreshadowing the legendary Jerry Glanville comment fifty-six years later.

After a few short speeches, including comments from Governor White, Cleveland Mayor Ray Miller spoke for about ten minutes during which the capacity crowd grew a bit restless. Following the playing of the "Star-Spangled Banner," Philadelphia second baseman Max Bishop, in his gray uniform and Italian-blue cap, stepped into the batter's box for the ceremonial first pitch, which Governor White would toss to Mayor Miller while baseball commissioner Kenesaw Mountain Landis played the role of umpire. White tossed a looper outside, and Landis couldn't decide if it was a ball or strike. A moment later the Indians (in their white wool uniforms with a large blue "C" sewn to the left breast and blue caps with a white stitched "C") took the field for the first time in what would be a long, stormy relationship between team and ballpark.

In addition to the circus atmosphere, this was a key game at the time. The Athletics and Indians were both pursuing the Yankees in the American League pennant race as they stood in second and third, respectively.

As Harder, the Cleveland starter in place of an ailing Wes Ferrell, fired the first pitch, he recalled that the ball was supposed to be saved as a memento for Governor White. But Bishop apparently didn't get that message. "I wound up and just laid that first pitch in there," Harder says in the *Cleveland Indians Encyclopedia*, "expecting that Bishop would take it, the umpire would make his call, toss the ball out of play, and we'd start over again. But Bishop took a helluva cut and hit a line drive into the left-field stands. We were lucky it went foul."

A few moments later Bishop slapped the first-ever hit at Cleveland Stadium, a single to right. *That* baseball eventually found its way into Alva Bradley's paws.

While Harder was brilliant on this day, his counterpart was even better. Robert Moses Grove—nicknamed "Lefty"—was one of the best pitchers in the game and had compiled a remarkable 31-4 record the year before. Grove went the distance and allowed just four Cleveland hits. The first was in the third inning off the bat of second baseman Bill Cissell.

Both pitchers came up big in the right moments. With Athletics on first and second with one out in the first, Harder struck out Al Simmons and Jimmy Foxx to get out of the jam. The Indians threatened in the third when a Cissell hit and a Bill Kamm sacrifice were followed by a ground out by Harder, putting Cissell at third with two down. Grove rallied to retire Dick Porter and end the inning. In the fifth Harder came up with another huge strikeout, this one of Mickey Cochrane with runners on first and third and two out.

Through seven innings each team had just four hits, all singles, and the game remained scoreless, although the Indians had missed a golden opportunity to score moments before. Earl Averill singled, and Joe Vosmik beat out a bunt to start things off in the bottom of the seventh, but a second sacrifice attempt by Eddie Morgan was extinguished by Grove. He scooped up the ball and tossed it to third to eliminate Averill, then whiffed Luke Sewell for the second out. Cissell returned to the plate for an attempt to add the first Cleveland Stadium RBI to his list of achievements for the day. He cranked a frozen rope into right, but at the last moment it hooked foul. A moment later Cissell grounded out to end the inning and the Indians' only legitimate scoring threat of the afternoon.

Just as he'd inked his name in Cleveland memory books with the first hit at the new park, Bishop once again took a step toward history in the eighth inning. He drew a walk from Harder, was sacrificed to second, and scored the first run in the Stadium on a Mickey Cochrane single that just eluded Harder's glove and bounced into center field. The Indians were then held scoreless in the eighth. Although Foxx cranked a double in the ninth for the first extra-base hit at Cleveland Stadium, Indians' reliever Oral Hildebrand got out of the jam.

Despite the fact that two of the best pitchers of the era were on the mound for their respective teams, another factor may have caused both clubs' offenses to struggle. Of the ten thousand fans in the center-field bleachers, all but seventeen were wearing white shirts and no coats. Many batters complained that they simply couldn't see the ball against that backdrop.

Appropriate for what would follow in this ballpark over the next sixty years, the final out of the game gleamed with irony. Morgan pounded Grove's final pitch deep into right field. At League Park, Morgan's shot would have sailed over the forty-foot wall and forced extra innings. Instead, Philadelphia's Bing Miller caught it just in front of the stands (there were no outfield fences until 1947) to conclude a 1-0 Athletics' triumph in as crisp a baseball contest as one could hope for.

"As long as we had to lose, I'm glad we were beaten the way we were," Peckinpaugh told the *Plain Dealer*. The Indians dropped to 58-42, 9½ games behind the Yankees. "The A's got that big break and they came through but we'll get 'em tomorrow."

Connie Mack also seemed to appreciate the carnival atmosphere. "If it were not for the fact that we're all in this game to win as often as we possibly can," he said to the *Plain Dealer*, "I would have liked to see the Indians finish in front, too. The fact that our team played the first game in such a stadium before such a crowd is a great compliment. It was a perfect day for baseball: the crowd was perfect and so was the stadium in all details."

This was true during the game, but afterward fans discovered the downfall to being a part of the largest crowd to attend a sporting event in American history: downtown Cleveland became one colossal traffic jam. Nearly 25,000 private automobiles, plus several thousand taxis, busses, and streetcars tried to maneuver through the streets at just past five that afternoon. The last car didn't leave the stadium parking lot until 6:30.

Despite the loss and the traffic, it certainly appeared to be a triumphant day for the city of Cleveland. For one thing, Indians' general manager Billy Evans estimated the gross from the first game at near $80,000, of which the Indians received $47,500.

That evening, the verdict was in, and Cleveland was beaming with pride. Kenesaw Mountain Landis called the new stadium "perfect." The *Plain Dealer* called it "the ultimate athletic facility in the country," and said, "it is the last word both in convenience for the spectator and in facility for games, athletics, and civic gatherings which are to be held there in the years to come."

Former *Plain Dealer* sports editor Henry Edwards also saw a bright future, but not just for the stadium: "I hope the day is not far away when Cleveland will fill that stadium for four World Series games," he said. Edwards' dream would come true, though for three games, not four, and not for another sixteen years.

At the same time, the natural comparisons were being made between the new yard and League Park:

"League Park . . . is wholly inadequate for big-time stuff," said *Plain Dealer* sports editor Sam Otis.

"As compared with today's stadium, that grand stand wasn't so magnificent after all," agreed Charles W. Mears, one of Otis' writers.

In reality, this miracle on the lake marked the beginning of a long and rather odd chapter in Indians' history. They played the remaining thirty-two home games of the 1932 season there, but problems loomed on the horizon.

First, the overall attendance for the 1932 season was actually less than the season before, when all the games were played at League Park, which had a much-smaller capacity of 21,414. In addition, many hitters complained that Municipal Stadium was simply too big. "You'd have to have a horse to play outfield here," an aging Babe Ruth once said, and, appropriately, the Babe never hit a home run at Cleveland Stadium.

The drainage system was found to be shoddy, and the dugouts would occasionally flood. Problems even arose in the stands, where forty-four pillars blocked views from hundreds of seats around the park, and with its location right on the lake the weather was usually quite unpredictable.

The Indians played the entire 1933 home schedule at the Stadium, and attendance was even lower than the last full year at League Park. Suddenly Bradley wasn't quite as proud of the reality of Cleveland Stadium as he'd been of the idea. He returned the Indians to League Park for the entire 1934 season and kept them there for all but one home game in 1935 and 1936. Between 1936 and 1946 the Indians would play a total of 415 games at brand-new Cleveland Stadium and 487 at League Park. "It was like we were on the road even when we were at home," Indians' shortstop and manager Lou Boudreau said in 1945.

As a result, it wasn't until 1942, eleven years after it was completed, that Cleveland Stadium finally turned a profit.

Naturally, city officials and voters who had footed the bill for this now "giant white elephant" were a bit miffed, and Bradley was heavily criticized for abandoning Cleveland's shining jewel. He agreed to have the team play a few games—generally on Sundays and holidays—at the Stadium in 1937 but would still hold the majority of home contests at League Park. The lights that had cost extra during construction in 1931 weren't switched on for a baseball game until 1939, when Bob Feller pitched a one-hitter against the Detroit Tigers in the park's first night game.

The Indians' locale crisis continued through the 1946 season, Bill Veeck's first as owner of the club. Unlike Bradley, Veeck didn't see a giant white elephant. He saw eighty thousand seats people would pay to sit in to watch a winning team. Following the final home game of 1946, a 5-3 loss to Detroit (perhaps *that* was the game that the TV show *Homefront*'s producers were referring to), Veeck nonchalantly announced his decision to move the team back to the Stadium full time for the 1947 season. They would stay there on a permanent basis for the next forty-six years.

Veeck's vision became reality a year later when the Indians set a major-league record by drawing 2.6 million fans during their world championship season of 1948. They also drew more than two million in 1949, then over a million each season from 1950 through 1955, although only half as many fans attended in the pennant-winning 1954 season as had in 1948. With the Indians racking up five second-place finishes to New York in the 1950s, attendance dwindled over the second half of the decade before soaring back over 1.4 million in 1959, when the Tribe challenged the White Sox down to the final weeks of the season.

Then came the dark times.

Cleveland suffered losing records in twenty-six of the next thirty-four seasons, and attendance reflected the fact. From 1960 to 1973 the Indians failed to draw a million fans in any season, and they managed it only three times between 1975 and 1985. Attendance hovered around the million mark for much of the late 1980s, then catapulted back over two million for the final season at the Stadium in 1993.

Cleveland Stadium ended up being the site of some of the worst baseball in America for three decades. It was the home of the now-infamous ten-cent beer night in 1974 that resulted in a drunken riot by fans and an Indians' forfeit to Texas. It was the home of a quartet of 100-loss teams and 17 different managers in 33 seasons. When it was to host its fourth and final All-Star Game in 1981, the midsummer's classic was postponed a month because of a players' strike. The Stadium became the flea market of Major League Baseball and a showcase for the sport's clearance-rack talent.

Six decades later, with their new locale start under way, the Indians hoped those days were ancient history, as a prime example of top-shelf talent stepped up to the plate to lead off the bottom of the third, rookie Manny Ramirez.

The Indians selected Ramirez in the thirteenth round of the 1991 draft, and he quickly carved his way through the minors. After lighting up opposing pitchers in Burlington and Kinston in 1991 and 1992, Ramirez started the 1993 season at AA Canton-Akron and hit .340 in eighty-nine games. He then moved to AAA Charlotte, where he hit .317 in forty games, and finished the season with the Indians. (He quickly gave Tribe fans a preview of what was to come when he spanked a pair of homers at Yankee Stadium in his second major-league game.) Ramirez was named Minor League Player of the Year by *Baseball America,* and after a spectacular spring he captured the starting spot in right field over Wayne Kirby for opening day 1994.

Now he stood at home plate in his first at-bat at Jacobs Field and took a fastball from Randy Johnson, high and outside for ball one. Ramirez then popped the second offering into right field, where Buhner made a routine catch for the first out.

The number-nine batter in the Cleveland lineup that day was one whom fans certainly recognized. At the same time they knew that his time as part of the leadership blazing the Indians into the Jacobs Field era had passed. Mark Lewis can always say he was in the first-ever starting lineup at Jacobs Field, but even he knew that it was due more to circumstance than destiny.

A Hamilton, Ohio, native, the Indians drafted Lewis with the second overall pick in 1988 as a high-percentage hitter and versatile infielder. After three seasons in the minors he broke in with the club with a vengeance in 1991. When starting shortstop Felix Fermin was placed on the disabled list with a strained calf muscle the last week of April, Lewis was called up to fill in. Like Manny Ramirez, Lewis made a smashing major-league debut. He singled off Nolan Ryan in his first at-bat and knocked in two runs in the game to begin a month-long campaign of smoking American League pitchers. He collected twelve multiple-hit performances in his first nineteen major-league games, and his batting average flirted with .400. Lewis moved to second base when Fermin returned in mid-May, but he couldn't keep up the pace he'd set. He was sent back to AAA Colorado Springs in late July, and even though he came back with the Indians in September and hit well, he still finished at just .264 for the year. Lewis returned to shortstop for the 1992 season and once again hit .264, but he spent most of 1993 at AAA Charlotte after getting beat out at short by Felix Fermin and at second by the emerging Baerga. With the signing of Omar Vizquel, Lewis had been relegated to a role as utility infielder.

"Everybody keeps asking me how it feels to be a utility player," Lewis told the *Plain Dealer* a few days before the opener. "I tell them I don't like being a utility player, but I want to play on this team. You make adjustments."

The reason right-handed Lewis, and not young phenomenon Jim Thome, started at third on this opening day was due to the six-foot-ten factor coming set on the mound. The left-handed Thome had struggled with southpaws in his limited major-league action, and facing someone like Randy Johnson on his first opening day could do serious damage to the young third baseman's confidence. Plus, Thome's defense was a question mark going into 1994. His range of snagging hard-hit balls was fine, but his throws to first were occasionally wild and off-line. Lewis was much steadier defensively, although he lacked the offensive threat that Thome already represented.

Lewis received a steady diet of fastballs from Johnson. The first missed, and the next two caught the corner to put the third baseman behind 1-and-2. With a high fastball to break the routine, Lewis fouled off three of the next four fastballs before Johnson finally came in with a curve on the eighth pitch, which Lewis grounded back to him. Johnson jogged toward first and underhanded the ball to Martinez for the second out.

Kenny Lofton then stepped in and picked up where he left off in the first inning, receiving his fifth straight ball from Johnson. But the gangly southpaw struck back and rang up Lofton without his ever taking the bat off his shoulder. A fastball zipped through the strike zone, and then a pair of curves fooled Lofton, who became Johnson's first strikeout victim of the season.

In the third, the Indians scored no runs on no hits, and there were no errors.

THE FOURTH

	1	2	3	4	5	6	7	8	9		R	H	E
SEATTLE	1	0	1								2	1	0
CLEVELAND	0	0	0								0	0	0

Is that Rocky Colavito in the middle in a *Tigers'* uniform? Unlikely as it might have seemed, this bizarre scenario came true two days before opening day 1960. (*Cleveland Press* Collection, Cleveland State University)

Reggie Jefferson quickly became the first out of the inning by pounding Dennis Martinez's first pitch into the ground toward short, where Omar Vizquel scooped it up and threw it to Eddie Murray.

Martinez then fell behind Dan Wilson 3-and-0 with a trio of curveballs. The fourth became strike one. Wilson popped the fifth pitch into shallow center, where Vizquel called off Carlos Baerga and Kenny Lofton and caught it ten feet out onto the grass for the second out.

Felix Fermin, Vizquel's counterpart this day in more ways than one, stepped in next. Seeing that Mark Lewis was playing back and off the bag at third, he attempted to lay down a bunt on the left side of the infield. He fouled back the first pitch, but Lewis got the message and scooted up a few steps before Martinez missed outside with a fastball for ball one. Fermin rocketed the third pitch down the first-base line, where it bounced off the heel of Murray's glove, knocked against his shin, and caromed into foul territory. Martinez raced to cover first, while Murray crawled over to the slow-rolling ball, picked it up, and fired off-balance from his knees to Martinez as Fermin reached the bag. Murray's toss sailed past Martinez into the infield, but Vizquel cut it off at the mound to keep Fermin from advancing. Murray's throw was ruled the first error in Jacobs Field history, and now with Rich Amaral coming up the Mariners had a baserunner for the third straight inning.

Martinez fell behind Amaral 3-and-0 with a pair of outside fastballs and a high curve. After getting another curve over for the first strike, he made two tosses to first to keep Fermin close, just as he had done after the first pitch of the at-bat. Amaral skied the fifth pitch to left field, where Albert Belle caught it to retire the side.

In the fourth, the Mariners scored no runs on no hits, and the Indians committed an error.

	1	2	3	4	5	6	7	8	9			R	H	E
SEATTLE	1	0	1	0								2	1	0
CLEVELAND	0	0	0									0	0	1

While opening day can be thought of as a glass bottle that contains the bright promise of spring bobbing in an ocean of optimism, it occasionally can also represent the widespread negativity of hostile seas. On this opening day in 1994, if Indians' fans were to trace the origins of their team's three-decade slump to one moment, most would pinpoint another opening day thirty-four years earlier. It was the day when, as sportswriter Terry Pluto would write years later, "A Slump of a Thousand Years Begins with One Loss."

Without question the most popular player on the Indians' roster during the late 1950s was a tall, dark, and handsome outfielder from New York by the name of Rocco Domenico Colavito. After first breaking in with the club in 1955—the same year young Cleveland pitching phenom Herb Score won the American League Rookie of the Year award—Rocky Colavito became a mainstay for the Indians for the next four seasons.

In his first full year in 1956 he hit twenty-one home runs and drove in sixty-five RBI, and those totals grew each of the next two years. He led the league with a .620 slugging percentage in 1958 to go along with 41 homers, 113 RBI, and a .303 batting average. In 1959 his average dropped to .257, but he hit 42 more round-trippers and knocked in 111 runs as the Tribe finished five games behind the pennant-winning Chicago White Sox. Colavito claimed status as a local legend on June 10, 1959, when he hit four home runs in one game in an 11-8 Indians' win over the Orioles in Baltimore. He became just the eighth major-league player to hit four in a game and only the third to accomplish the feat in consecutive at-bats. Fan clubs had organized to follow Colavito's heroics, and he seemed to represent the all-American baseball player. As it turned out, that reputation would be his downfall in Cleveland.

A few weeks after Hank Greenberg was fired in 1957 after eight seasons as general manager, the Indians hired Frank Lane, then general manager of the St. Louis Cardinals, to take his place. The Tribe brass knew that Lane wasn't afraid to shake things up on his team and hoped that he could guide the Indians back to where they had been earlier in the decade, culminating with the 1954 pennant-winner. Little did they know that Lane would plant a tumor in the Indians' franchise that would take thirty-five years to remove.

Between his first day on the job (November 12, 1957) and his last (January 3, 1961) Lane made 59 transactions involving 120 players. Very few were shrewd; most were downright ridiculous. He was the man who traded Roger Maris to Kansas City for Vic Power and Woodie Held three years before Maris broke Babe Ruth's single-season home-run record with the New York Yankees. Lane traded Early Wynn, Bobby Avila, Vic Wertz, Larry Doby, and Minnie Minoso, to name a few of the notables, and even traded his manager, Joe Gordon, for Detroit skipper Jimmy Dykes in 1960.

But it was another deal Lane had made with Detroit earlier that year for which he will always be known in Cleveland. If it was not the move that hexed the team with a generation-long curse, then it certainly was one of the biggest public relations gaffs in Cleveland sports history.

On April 17, 1960, two days before the season was to begin, the Indians played the White Sox in an exhibition game in Memphis, Tennessee. Colavito hit a home run in his first at-bat, and he reached first on a fielder's choice in his second. Manager Gordon came out of the dugout and informed Colavito that he had just been traded to the Detroit Tigers for outfielder Harvey Kuenn. Colavito was taken out of the game, stunned. He told Herb Score, his roommate, who initially thought he was kidding.

A few hours later, Lane announced the deal to the media at a 4 P.M. press conference.

"What we've done is this," he explained, "we've given up forty home runs for forty doubles. We've added fifty singles and taken away fifty strikeouts. That about sums it up."

Lane went on to say that he and Gordon both believed home runs were overrated and that Kuenn would provide more offensively than the man who had produced 308 runs in the past three seasons. "I'm perfectly happy about the deal," Kuenn said in the *Plain Dealer*. "I think the Indians have a good chance to win the pennant, and I've always liked to play in Cleveland."

True, Kuenn had won the AL batting title the year before with a .353 average and led the league with 198 hits and 42 doubles, but he hit just nine home runs with seventy-one RBI. Plus, Kuenn was thirty years old; Colavito was twenty-six. "I hated to give up a fine young ballplayer like Rocky," Lane told reporters, "but I feel we'll have a better chance to win the pennant with Kuenn."

There had been rumors swirling about a potential Kuenn-for-Colavito trade all spring, since Colavito had held out of training camp during his annual contract negotiations with Lane. He signed the first week of March for less than he wanted, because he didn't want to hurt the team's chances for the 1960 pennant, and the rumors died off.

But Lane just didn't like Colavito. He didn't think Colavito was a true ballplayer because he didn't fit the brash, outgoing stereotype, and he blamed Colavito for the Indians' failure to win the '59 pennant. Colavito's late-season slump *had* proved costly, as the Indians struggled to catch Chicago, but they never would have been in contention without him.

Many sportswriters felt the move made the Tigers an instant contender for the World Series. Naturally, fan reaction in Cleveland was a staggering 9-to-1 against the deal, according to a *Plain Dealer* survey. "I'll never go to the ballpark again," said fan Robert Intorcio. "Frank Lane just threw away the pennant," agreed fellow Tribe rooter William Cotner.

Making matters worse, the Indians would open the regular season at home two days later against the Tigers. Cleveland sports fans wouldn't see anything like this again for thirty-three years, when popular Browns' quarterback Bernie Kosar was cut because head coach Bill Belichick and owner Art Modell preferred to start unproven Todd Philcox.

When the Indians' plane arrived at Hopkins Airport just after 11 the night of the trade, about 300 fans were on hand to greet them. A sign had been hung near the gate that read, "Up with Rock, Down with Trader Lane."

Lane was the first person off the plane, and it looked as though he planned on entering the witness protection program. He emerged from the darkness in a raincoat and sunglasses. Colavito was next off the plane, and he received a hearty ovation from the late-night partition.

"I hate to leave Cleveland because the fans have been so good to me," he told the *Plain Dealer*. "I really love those people and always will. Nothing will ever change that."

With a day off between the Colavito trade and opening day, Lane needed something to do. So he traded Herb Score to Chicago for Barry Latman.

"We simply reached the point where we felt Herb could not win for the Indians," Lane explained to the *Plain Dealer*. "We would not have traded him if we felt otherwise."

Score probably represented the ultimate "couldabeen" in Indians' history. After an incredible 1955 debut in which he won sixteen games with an ERA of 2.85 in 227 innings, he was even better in 1956, winning twenty with a 2.53 ERA and five complete-game shutouts. Most impressive was that he led the American League in strikeouts both seasons with 245 and 263, respectively. He was expected to be one of the best pitchers in baseball for a long, long time.

But after a line drive off the bat of New York's Gil McDougald struck him in the eye in May 1957, Score's comeback was halted by a shoulder injury, and he was never the same again. He pitched just forty-one innings in 1958, and although he was healthy enough to be a full-time starter again in 1959, he'd compiled a 9-11 record with a 4.71 ERA and just 147 strikeouts.

Still Score was very popular in Cleveland. He had fan clubs of his own, and, had the trade been made on any other day, it would have been huge news. But since it was made just hours after the Colavito deal, it received relatively little notice.

The *Plain Dealer* reported that Colavito was on the phone being interviewed by a New York sportswriter when the Score trade came over the wire. The writer told him about the trade, and Colavito was silent for a moment.

"You're kidding," he said.

The writer assured him, no, it was the truth, and there was a long silence on the other end.

"That man must be crazy," Colavito finally replied.

Latman was getting a haircut in his hometown of Hammond, Indiana, when he heard of his trade over the radio. Shocked, he jumped in his chair, and the barber let out a yelp as he nearly cut off Latman's ear.

From Hollywood comedian Bob Hope expressed concern about coming to Cleveland for a dinner in his honor later in the week. "I'm afraid Frank Lane might trade me," he joked.

And despite the front-office shenanigans, opening day was right around the corner. "If they haven't traded Municipal Stadium for Comiskey Park, there will be a baseball game down there at three this afternoon," George Barmann of the *Plain Dealer* wrote in Tuesday's edition.

Lane managed to keep the stadium in Cleveland that day, and one of the oddest and longest opening games in Indians' history began that afternoon.

There was actually some booing of Colavito during the pregame introductions and each of his at-bats, while Kuenn received a surprisingly enthusiastic welcome. "They treated me nice," Colavito said to the *Plain Dealer*. "I can't expect them to kiss me. I'm on the other side now—the enemy."

The game itself seemed like an anticlimax, almost a two-man show, and rarely is there such a thing in baseball. Indians' fans would have known for certain they were doomed for a thousand years of agony if Colavito had gone 4-for-4 and hit the game-winning home run while Kuenn went hitless, but that's not what happened. In fact almost the opposite happened, as 52,756 fans, Cleveland's largest opening-day crowd in seven years, would attest.

It was Colavito who had the lousy game—the worst of his career, he'd say later. It all began when manager Jimmy Dykes misspelled his name on the Detroit lineup card, which listed him as "Covolita." Colavito proceeded to go 0-for-6 with four strikeouts. He also committed two errors in right, one of which had a huge impact on the game.

"If those fans in the stands thought it was a long day, how about me?" Colavito told reporters after the game. "I had to suffer through it. All they had to do was watch it."

Kuenn, meanwhile, went 2-for-7 with a double, and he made some nifty catches in center.

After ten scoreless innings, in which Cleveland starter Gary Bell and Tigers' hurler Frank Lary went the whole way, the Tigers surged ahead 2-0 in the eleventh on a two-run single by Neil Chrisley. In the bottom of the inning, Colavito, who had lost a Tito Francona flare in the sun in the ninth, misjudged a drive off the bat of Russ Nixon that resulted in a double and put the tying runs in scoring position for pinch hitter Jim Piersall. Piersall came through with a two-out, two-run single that tied the game and sent it to the twelfth.

In the fourteenth Kuenn pulled a leg muscle running out a ground ball and had to leave the game. An inning later Cleveland's Jim "Mudcat" Grant surrendered a walk and a double, and Johnny Kleppstein replaced him, only to walk Charley Maxwell. Bob Tiefenauer then came in and gave up a bases-loaded single to Al Kaline for two runs. The inning ended when Colavito grounded into a double play.

Although Vic Power doubled with one out in the bottom of the inning, Detroit reliever Pete Burnside struck out the side and after four hours and fifty-four minutes the Tigers won, 4-2, in fifteen innings. At the time, it was the longest opener in major-league history.

The outcome of the two-man duel favored the Indians on this day. "The showdown battle between Rocky Colavito and Harvey Kuenn, with Frank Lane's scalp as the prize, was strictly no contest," wrote *Plain Dealer* sports editor Gordon Cobbledick, "Kuenn won it hands down."

But that sentiment would prove to be a one-day illusion foreshadowed by a reminder of Lane's track record that afternoon. At Fenway Park Roger Maris collected four hits, including a pair of home runs and four RBI, as the Yankees defeated the Red Sox, 8-4. Maris would go on to hit thirty-nine home runs and lead the league with 112 RBI in 1960 before his historic 1961 campaign.

The next day the Tigers defeated the Indians again, 6-4, on the strength of a three-run home run by Rocky Colavito. Later that season the Tigers would win back-to-back thrillers over the Indians in Cleveland, the first on a tenth-inning home run and the second on a game-winning double—both by Rocky Colavito.

Lane was fired following the 1960 season and was replaced by Gabe Paul, who kept the position through most of the dark years that followed in the sixties, seventies, and eighties.

Although neither team really benefited from the Colavito-Kuenn trade (in 1960 the Indians finished fourth and the Tigers sixth, both with losing records), the Tigers eventually got the larger portion of the wishbone. Colavito hit 139 homers and drove in 430 runs in four seasons in Detroit, while Kuenn's average dropped to .308 in 1960 with nine homers and fifty-four RBI. Kuenn was traded that December to the San Francisco Giants for aging pitcher Johnny Antonelli and hard-hitting outfielder Willie Kirkland, when Lane suddenly decided that his team needed another power hitter. Kuenn would never again hit close to his 1959 average nor collect as many hits. He moved from the Giants to the Cubs to the Phillies in the next six years and retired following the 1966 season.

Colavito, meanwhile, was traded to the Kansas City Athletics in 1964 before returning to Cleveland the following year in probably the worst trade the team had made since the first time he was dealt. Desperately seeking some good publicity after rumors leaked of the team's interest in moving to Seattle following the 1964 season, the Indians traded young prospects Tommy John, a left-handed pitcher, and speedy outfielder Tommie Agee in a three-team deal with Chicago and Kansas City. John would go on to win 286 career games after he left the Indians and to pitch in three World Series with the Yankees and Dodgers. Agee became a valuable member of the Miracle Mets team that won the 1969 World Series.

Although this trade brought the beloved Rocky back to Cleveland, at thirty-one years old he was not the same player who had left five years before. He hit a respectable .287 with twenty-six homers and led the league with 108 RBI in 1965, then clubbed thirty round-trippers the following year as his average slipped to .238. Midway through the 1967 season, Colavito was traded to Chicago for Jim King and Marv Staehle. Colavito finished his career with the Yankees in 1968, never having reached a World Series.

The afterthought Score-Latman deal of mid-April 1960 turned out to do little more than agitate Cleveland fans. Latman went 7-7 in 1960 and had a nice '61 season, going 13-5 with an ERA of 4.02. He remained a fulltime starter in Cleveland in 1962 and 1963, even though he compiled an unimpressive record of 15-25. He was traded to Los Angeles in December 1963 for Leon Wagner and finished his career with Houston three years later.

Score, meanwhile, went 5-10 with the White Sox in 1960, despite a respectable 3.72 ERA, but he saw little action the next two seasons due to injury and retired in 1962. He finished his career with a 55-46 record and a 3.36 ERA. In 1964 Score joined the Indians' radio broadcasting team and would become a living legacy as the voice of the Tribe over the next three decades before retiring from the booth following the 1997 season.

So did the first Colavito trade truly curse the Indians?

In the twelve seasons before he was traded, the team compiled a record of 1,090-757, a winning percentage of .590, with two pennants and one world championship. In the thirty-four seasons following the trade and leading up to the opening of Jacobs Field, they compiled a record of 2,516-2,903, a winning percentage of .464, with one third-place finish. Certainly other factors were involved, but the

trade of Rocky Colavito on that fateful April afternoon in 1960 seemed to symbolize the years of frustration to follow.

After thirty-four of those years Cleveland fans were ready for a change of
fortune.

Leading off the bottom of the fourth, Vizquel seemed ready for a free pass to
first for the second straight at-bat when he went ahead of Randy Johnson 3-and-
0, fooling him with bunt attempts on the first two pitches. Vizquel got the green
light on the fourth pitch, which he popped off the inside part of the bat into left
field. Eric Anthony caught it for the first out, bringing up Carlos Baerga.

Baerga took two curves, one for a strike over the outside corner and one a bit
outside for a ball, before breaking his bat on the third curve and rolling a slow
grounder to Fermin at short. Fermin scooped it up and threw it on to Tino
Martinez to retire Baerga.

While Baerga was chewing on Johnson's offerings, the president of the United
States was enjoying the culinary benefits of opening day. With Art Modell, act-
ing baseball commissioner Bud Selig, and White House communications director George Stephanopoulos hobnobbing nearby, Clinton nibbled on a hot dog
just outside of Richard Jacobs' loge high above home plate, gazing out at the
new ballpark. Eighty-four years after William Howard Taft became the first president to throw out the first pitch on opening day, Clinton proved that some things
don't change much over time.

Albert Belle then stepped in for the first time since he failed to cash in on the
Indians' only scoring opportunity in the first by grounding out with Vizquel at
second. Trying to break Johnson's string of retiring ten straight batters, Belle
went ahead 2-and-0 when a curve and slider missed out and in, respectively. He
then fouled back a pair of fastballs to even the count. On the fifth pitch Belle
smacked a solid grounder to the right side that streaked between Martinez's legs
and into right field. Although this ball was hit harder, the play bore an eerie
similarity to Mookie Wilson's nubber that somehow found its way through Bill
Buckner's legs in Game Six of the 1986 World Series. Martinez was awarded an
error for the miscue, the second of the ballgame.

With Eddie Murray in the box trying to capitalize on the mistake, for the
third time in the inning, Johnson fell behind 2-and-0 when a pair of fastballs
dipped low. He came back with another fastball, this one at the knees for strike
one, then Murray knocked another slowly to Fermin, who tossed to Rich Amaral
at second to force Belle and end the inning.

In the fourth, the Indians scored no runs on no hits, and the Mariners committed an error.

THE FIFTH

	1	2	3	4	5	6	7	8	9			R	H	E
SEATTLE	1	0	1	0								2	1	1
CLEVELAND	0	0	0	0								0	0	1

Frank Robinson hits the most memorable home run in Indians' history on opening day 1975. (*Cleveland Press* Collection, Cleveland State University)

Despite what would transpire at Jacobs Field in forthcoming seasons, it was unreasonable for anyone to think on April 4, 1994, that home runs would be the only form of base hits at the new ballpark.

Filling in for the injured Edgar Martinez at third, Mike Blowers smacked the first traditional hit when he blooped a first-pitch Dennis Martinez fastball into right field for a single. With Ken Griffey Jr. stepping up next, Martinez had to be especially careful—he couldn't put his club in any deeper a hole if the Indians were to stage a comeback.

He missed low with a curve on the first pitch but came back and got Griffey to whiff on two straight—the first a dazzling offspeed pitch and the second an inside curve. After fouling off another offspeed toss Griffey nubbed a breaking ball just in front of the plate, where Sandy Alomar dug it out and tossed it to Eddie Murray at first for out number one, while Blowers moved on to second. Frustrated after being badly fooled by Martinez for the second straight at-bat, Griffey spiked his batting helmet on his way back to the dugout.

With Blowers now in scoring position Martinez had to again be cautious as Jay Buhner stepped in. He missed low with a curveball on the first pitch before Buhner belted an offspeed ball into center, where Kenny Lofton was waiting for it. Lofton caught it for the second out and quickly fired to third, but Blowers wasn't going anywhere.

Even with Griffey and Buhner, Seattle's two primary power outlets, out of the way, Martinez had to face the man who was responsible for the Mariners' 2-0 lead. Eric Anthony had knocked in Edgar Martinez with a sacrifice fly in the first and then hit the first home run in Jacobs Field history in the third. If Martinez wasn't careful, the score could easily be Eric Anthony 4, Indians 0.

Martinez went ahead 0-and-1 with a fastball that nipped the outside corner and then missed outside for ball one. Anthony tried to hold back on an offspeed toss on the third pitch but instead checked the ball fair down the first-base line. Martinez and Alomar both raced for it, but Alomar got there first and then made the most athletic play of the game thus far. He grabbed it with his bare right hand and then, fading away, made an underhand lob over the streaking Anthony right to Murray to retire the side.

With Martinez only throwing eleven pitches, the fifth would prove to be the shortest inning of the afternoon. And although he was in a groove, Martinez's pitch count was becoming a factor. He had thrown eighty pitches: forty-five strikes and thirty-five balls. Conversely, Randy Johnson waltzed out to take his place on the mound, having thrown only fifty-seven pitches. Unfortunately for the Indians, he too was in a groove.

In the fifth, the Mariners scored no runs on one hit, and there were no errors.

	1	2	3	4	5	6	7	8	9			R	H	E
SEATTLE	1	0	1	0	0							2	2	1
CLEVELAND	0	0	0	0								0	0	1

Naturally, when a team is a perennial doormat over a long period of time, opening day is not as exciting for its fans as it is in cities where teams contend for the pennant each year. But even for teams as bad as the Indians were throughout the sixties, seventies, and eighties, opening day symbolized a fresh start, producing a kind of thinking not possible once the reality of the regular season sets in. Opening day brims with optimism as the one day of the year when anything is possible and, in the standings at least, everybody's equal.

Baseball took its first steps toward equality on the field when Jackie Robinson debuted with the Brooklyn Dodgers in 1947, but it would be nearly three more decades before a black man was hired to manage a major-league team. Just as the Indians had been pioneers by bringing Larry Doby up as the American League's first black player a few months after Robinson's appearance, they would be the first to cross the color barrier in the hiring of a manager.

Actually, hiring may not be the correct word. Promoting describes the situation better. One day after Ken Aspromonte was fired, following the 1974 season, designated hitter Frank Robinson was named as the team's new player-manager, Cleveland's first since Lou Boudreau.

Robinson was nearing the end of a long and brilliant career, and becoming a manager seemed the likely next step. He broke into the majors with the Reds in 1956 and spent ten impressive years in Cincinnati, hitting .300 five times and thirty-plus home runs seven times, and he captured the National League Most Valuable Player award in 1961. After the 1965 season the Reds figured the thirty-year old Robinson would soon run out of gas and traded him to Baltimore that December for Milt Pappas, Jack Baldschun, and Dick Simpson. In an era when the Reds were loading up with young talent that would blossom into a National League dynasty in the 1970s, this trade would prove to be one of the worst in franchise history. What's more, it is frightening to think what the Big Red Machine of the early 1970s might have been with Frank Robinson in the lineup.

In 1966 Robinson proved that he was far from being out of gas, earning AL MVP honors with a .316 average, forty-nine home runs, and 133 RBI, then helping the Orioles sweep the Dodgers in the World Series. He went on to be a stalwart in Baltimore through the early 1970s and led the Orioles to three more pennants. It's ironic that following the second of those pennant runs, Robinson faced his old team, the Reds, in the 1970 World Series. He hit two homers and drove in four runs in Baltimore's five-game triumph. By that year, all three of the players for whom he'd been traded were no longer with Cincinnati.

Robinson was traded to Los Angeles following the 1971 season and then to California the year after that. The Indians acquired him from the Angels in September 1974 for Ken Suarez, Rusty Torres, and cash. Robinson appeared in only fifteen games with Cleveland before being named manager. "Now that it has happened," said baseball commissioner Bowie Kuhn at the press conference, "I'm not going to get up and shout that this is something for baseball to be exceptionally proud of, because it is so long overdue." Robinson said that his only regret that day was that Jackie Robinson (no relation) wasn't alive to see it. Robinson died of a heart attack in the fall of 1972.

Frank Robinson's hiring marked a historic day for baseball, but probably less so than Robinson's managerial debut six months later.

Coming off a 77-85 season, expectations were about the same as usual for the 1975 Indians. But for one crisp spring day, the city of Cleveland, starved for something good on the diamond, got to see what baseball magic was all about.

The Indians (decked in their infamous 1970s' red home uniforms) were hosting the New York Yankees, a team enduring its own stretch of ineptitude, to kick off the season on April 8. Hundreds of media representatives and 56,715 fans piled into Cleveland Stadium to witness baseball history, but as Bob Dolgan of the Plain Dealer would write, "Thirty years from now a minimum of one million people will tell their grandchildren they were present."

In an *Akron Beacon Journal* article commemorating the twenty-fifth anniversary of his debut, Frank Robinson recalled the morning of the game. As he prepared to make history simply by standing in the dugout, Cleveland general manager Phil Seghi bumped into his new manager.

"Are you going to put yourself in the lineup?" Seghi asked.

Probably not, Robinson said. He hadn't batted much during spring training because of all his added duties as manager. He had told Cleveland sportswriters the day before that he was probably fifteen to twenty at-bats short of being really ready, but that he was "not hitting the ball too badly."

"You have to do it," Seghi replied. "You'll do something special. You'll rise to the occasion."

Robinson took Seghi's advice and decided to pencil himself in as the Indians' designated hitter, more as a ceremonial gesture than anything else. He figured that he could help set the tone for the kind of team he wanted by moving a runner or doing something fundamentally sound at the plate. Robinson would appear in only forty-eight other games that season, his second-to-last as a player.

Seghi had one more piece of pre-game advice for his manager.

"Why don't you hit a homer the first time you go to the plate?" he suggested. Robinson laughed him off.

"You've got to be kidding," he told Seghi.

There was already enough drama on this day without Robinson trying to add to it. For example, Rachel Robinson, Jackie Robinson's widow, threw out the first pitch on a rudely cold afternoon with a temperature near thirty-five degrees.

"I want to congratulate you for honoring yourselves by being the first to take this historic step," she told the crowd before the game. "I've wished, since I was asked to do this, that Jackie could be here, and I'm sure in many ways he is."

Gaylord Perry, the Cleveland starting pitcher that day, held the Yankees scoreless in the first, and after Oscar Gamble popped out to lead off the Indians' half, Frank Robinson stepped to the plate for the first time as a player-manager.

"I was kind of numb walking up to home plate," Robinson told the *Beacon Journal* in 2000. "In the batter's box, I said hello to the catcher [Thurman Munson] and the umpire [Nestor Chylak], and I thought I was in control."

But New York pitcher George "Doc" Medich demonstrated that although the day was special for Robinson and the sport of baseball in general, he wasn't going to hand the man of the hour an opportunity to make things even more memorable.

Medich went ahead 0-and-2 without Robinson's moving. Robinson barely fouled off the third pitch then stepped out of the box. He realized that Medich was not just trying to strike him out, but he was trying to embarrass Robinson on his special day. Suddenly the competitive nature of Frank Robinson gonged like a giant alarm clock. After fouling off another pitch, Robinson took a pair outside to even the count before Medich came back with a fastball over the outside corner.

At 2:21 P.M., Robinson swung and belted a line drive that scorched into the outfield and landed deep in the left-field stands. Just as Phil Seghi suggested, Frank Robinson had risen to the occasion and done something special.

After jumping through hoops for the media circus that had been following him around and asking him, "So what's it like to be the first black manager?" Robinson had replied, "Just fine, thank you," with one of the most dramatic moments in baseball history.

It was Robinson's 2,901st career hit and his 575th career homer, but it took a few moments for it to sink in as he rounded the bases. "At first there was nothing running through my mind, really," he told the *Cleveland Press,* "but by the time I got to third base, I thought to myself, 'Wow, will miracles ever cease?'"

As Robinson reached home plate and the crowd was going wild, he tipped his cap to his wife, Barbara, in the stands and then was mobbed by his teammates.

One of the first Indians to congratulate Robinson was Perry, who hadn't gotten along very well with Robinson during spring training. He embraced Robinson after he crossed home plate, and for the moment all previous misunderstandings between the pair were washed away.

The Indians went on to rally from a 3-1 deficit and defeat the Yankees 5-3, led by Tribe first baseman Boog Powell, who went 3-for-3 with a home run. When the game was over, Perry, who went the distance for the 199th victory of his career, and Robinson embraced once again. Robinson had returned Perry's newfound respect by leaving him in the game following a rough second inning and then again in the ninth when the Yankees brought the tying run to the plate in Thurman Munson. Munson had grounded back to Perry, who threw him out as the crowd exploded into a jet-engine level roar. It was the final subplot to a Hollywood kind of day.

"Right now I feel better than I have after anything I've done in baseball," Robinson told the *Cleveland Press.* "Take all the pennants, the personal awards, the World Series, the All-Star games, and this moment is the greatest. . . . It was unbelievable. If I could have asked God for a good day, I never would have asked for something like this and expected it to happen. Everything was all I could ask for."

"There wasn't one single disappointment for me, not one," added Seghi. "It was the kind of day, the kind of game, you only dream about, like Alice in Wonderland."

As was always the case in Cleveland since the Indians were swept by the New York Giants in the 1954 World Series, that fantasyland feeling didn't stick around for long. Robinson's first team went 79-80 and finished fourth, 15 1/2 games behind Boston in the AL East. The 1976 Indians weren't much better, going 81-78 and finishing fourth in Robinson's final year as a player. Still adjusting to the notion that few of his players were even close to being as talented as he was, Robinson came under fire from management and the fans. After beginning the season as manager in 1977, when the team got off to a 26-31 start, Robinson was replaced by coach Jeff Torborg.

Robinson went on to become the National League's first black skipper when he was hired to manage the San Francisco Giants in 1981. After four seasons on the bay, he returned to Baltimore as a coach and took charge of the Orioles six games into the 1988 season. He got off to a bit of a rocky start as the Orioles began the year with a major-league record twenty-one consecutive losses, but he pulled off one of the most impressive turnarounds in baseball history when the 1989 Orioles finished just two games behind Toronto in the AL East.

There were two interesting connections between Robinson's historic opening day in 1975 and Jacobs Field's first opening day in 1994. The first was the starting second baseman for New York, Sandy Alomar Sr., whose son would catch the first pitch at Jacobs Field. The second was the Yankee left fielder who had turned and watched Robinson's home run sail over his head and into the seats. It was Lou Piniella.

Nineteen years later Piniella again found himself in Cleveland on opening day with his team leading going into the bottom of the fifth inning, although this time as a manager. In the 1975 opener Boog Powell had tied the game in the fourth with a homer, and the Indians went on to score two in the seventh for the win. Piniella was hoping this time his lead would hold up.

After Randy Johnson jumped ahead of Candy Maldonado 0-and-2 to lead off the bottom of the fifth, he entered a rare, brief period in which he seemed unable to throw strikes consistently. Maldonado took two fastballs that missed and a curve in the dirt to push the count full before fouling another low curve into the seats along the first-base line. On Johnson's seventh pitch, Maldonado cracked a fastball sharply to Fermin at short, who then fired to Tino Martinez for the first out.

Johnson again jumped ahead 0-and-2 on Sandy Alomar but then missed high with a curve Alomar didn't even have to think about swinging at. After Alomar fouled back a tough fastball on the fourth pitch, Johnson again missed the target badly when a curve sailed to the backstop to even the count. Clearly flustered, he missed with a pair of fastballs high and outside, and Alomar became the Indians' fourth baserunner of the day on Johnson's third walk.

Before he knew it Johnson was down 3-and-0 to Manny Ramirez after a slider dipped low, a fastball floated outside, and a curve turned high. Johnson finally broke the string at six consecutive balls with a perfect breaking pitch to set up the fifth toss. Ramirez pounded a slider toward short, where Fermin fielded it, took two large gallops to tag second, and then fired across to Martinez to complete the first double play at Jacobs Field.

Johnson had survived his streak of wildness, and the Indians had to know they wouldn't get many more opportunities like it.

In the fifth, the Indians scored no runs on no hits, and there were no errors.

THE SIXTH

	1	2	3	4	5	6	7	8	9		R	H	E
SEATTLE	1	0	1	0	0						2	2	1
CLEVELAND	0	0	0	0	0						0	0	1

Indians' manager Mike Hargrove (left) argues with second-base umpire Al Clark after a controversial call in the sixth inning on opening day. (*Akron Beacon Journal*)

As Tino Martinez stepped into the batter's box to lead off the sixth, some five hundred feet away, Eric Plunk toed the rubber in the center-field bullpen as the first reliever to ever warm up at Jacobs Field. But with the way Dennis Martinez pitched in the sixth (much as he had in the fifth), it didn't appear that Mike Hargrove would be making any phone calls from the dugout soon.

Dennis sandwiched a curveball over the outside corner between a pair that missed, then he got Tino to flail at a breaking ball that sank out of the zone for strike two. The Martinez on the mound then finished off the Martinez in the box on the next pitch, a splendid offspeed toss Tino couldn't time with his swing. He became Dennis's second strikeout victim.

After Reggie Jefferson laid off a high breaking ball on his first pitch a moment later, the twenty-five-year-old Floridian spiked an outside pitch toward second, where Carlos Baerga had to run hard to catch up with it. He did so a few feet to the right of second but couldn't get a good grip on the ball when he turned to throw. As a result Baerga double-clutched before throwing, and the ball ended up bouncing before it got to Eddie Murray at first. By that time Jefferson had beaten the toss by two steps, and for the second straight inning Martinez would have to deal with a baserunner with less than two out.

Realizing that with the way Randy Johnson was pitching, a three-run lead might be insurmountable, Martinez jumped ahead of Dan Wilson 0-and-2 with a pair of fastballs over the outside corner. A third heater sailed high, and Wilson fouled off a fourth into the first-base seats. Martinez came back with a breaking ball on his fifth hurl, which Wilson pounded into center. Lofton raced back and gathered it in a step onto the rubberized warning track for the second out. Jefferson stayed at first.

Felix Fermin stepped into the box and quickly flared an inside fastball twenty feet into the air. Baerga caught it between first and second, retiring the side.

For the second straight inning Dennis Martinez looked like the pitcher he had been in Montreal and proved to the Cleveland fans just getting to know him that the first two innings of the game were not what he was all about.

In the sixth, the Mariners scored no runs on one hit, and there were no errors.

	1	2	3	4	5	6	7	8	9			R	H	E
SEATTLE	1	0	1	0	0	0						2	3	1
CLEVELAND	0	0	0	0	0							0	0	1

The baseball season is long, consisting of the most regular-season games of any professional sport in America. Opening day is just the tip of the iceberg, but it's often taken to be representative of what's to come in the spring and summer months.

Two years before this game at Jacobs Field, Indians' fans experienced an opening day that would go down as one of the most bizarre in club history. Although many didn't realize it at the time, Cleveland's 1992 home opener represented not only the forthcoming season but the previous thirty or so as well. It was The Opening Day That Wouldn't End.

From the get-go it seemed that the Indians were begging for something quirky to happen. After opening the season in Baltimore by losing two of three to the Orioles as they christened their new ballpark at Camden Yards, the Indians began their weekend series with the Boston Red Sox on a Saturday afternoon, the first time in seven years that Cleveland held its home opener on a Saturday. The teams would then play a doubleheader Sunday before the Detroit Tigers came to town on Monday.

Packed into Cleveland Stadium were 65,813 fans for what would be the largest opening-day crowd in baseball that year and the largest to see a major-league game in four seasons. Not much more than the magic of opening day could explain the big turnout.

The Indians were coming off the worst season in their history, and things didn't look much better for 1992. Mike Hargrove was beginning his first full year as manager, standing on a one-year contract that may as well have been a trap door if the '92 Indians were anything like the '91 version. There were several promising new faces in the lineup, including rookie Kenny Lofton and recently acquired Paul Sorrento making their Cleveland debuts, but for many in the crowd this day was clearly more suited for celebrating the return of spring than the return of the Tribe. And why not? For the first time in years, it actually felt like spring in Cleveland on opening day. The temperature climbed to near seventy degrees, and all appeared right with the world, even on the diamond.

As the fanfare of the pregame festivities finally wound down and lefty Dennis Cook prepared to fire the first pitch of the game to Wade Boggs, a sign came down from the heavens (over from the grandstand anyway) that seemed to be a prelude of what was to come.

An exotic dancer named Lulu Divine raced out toward the mound and planted a kiss on Cook's cheek before she was escorted out of the park and into a nearby jail cell. Cook shook it off, and at 1:43 P.M. on April 11, 1992, fired a fastball strike past Boggs to the roaring approval of the crowd. Opening day and all the optimism that came with it had finally arrived.

Much of that optimism was shattered a moment later when Boggs roped a double up the alley on Cook's second pitch. Two batters later the Red Sox led, 1-0, and after three innings things were back to normal in Cleveland, as Boston led by five. After seeing their team lose 105 games in every possible way imaginable the year before, Cleveland fans were used to it.

However, slowly but surely, the Indians started to show signs of life. After Cook was removed following 2⅔ troublesome innings, the Cleveland bullpen stepped up and extinguished the Boston bats. Rod Nichols got the Indians through the fourth, then Ted Power relieved him to toss three hitless innings. Meanwhile the Cleveland offense was gradually waking up. They scraped together a run in the fourth, then after Mark Lewis doubled in the fifth Lofton singled to cut the Boston lead to three. A double by Glenallen Hill scored Lofton next to make it 5-3.

In the seventh, Boston's Tom Bolton, pitching in relief of starter Joe Hesketh, loaded the bases and was replaced by Greg Harris. Albert Belle lifted a sacrifice fly to score Lofton from third, and after Mark Whiten walked, Sorrento hit a screamer down the first-base line that seemed destined to clear the bases and turn the game around. But Boston first baseman Mo Vaughn made a great stop and threw Sorrento out at first. The fielder's choice scored Hill to tie the game, but had the ball gotten by Vaughn, the Indians could have held a two-run lead with six outs to go.

The Cleveland fans were suddenly energized. Maybe this team wasn't a whole lot better than last year's, but they'd rallied back from a five-run deficit to create a whole new ballgame. No one could know how true that expression would prove to be.

Neither team scored in the eighth or ninth, and they plunged into extra innings as the late afternoon sun began to nestle into Lake Erie. The light grew dimmer as the game grew longer. The Indians and Red Sox fought through the tenth, eleventh, and twelfth innings without scoring.

Sometimes odd circumstances make baseball fans do odd things. With one out in the bottom of the thirteenth, Sandy Alomar doubled, bringing Dave Rohde, who'd replaced Tony Perezchica, who'd replaced Alex Cole, who'd replaced Brook Jacoby, to the plate. What was left of the throng of fans *really* wanted to go home by this time and showed it by chanting "Roh-de! Roh-de!"

The career-.158 hitter didn't get a chance to be the opening-day hero, since Boston's Danny Darwin intentionally walked him to face Lewis, for whom the insanity of this game was not a new experience. His first-ever professional game, when he was a member of Class A Burlington in 1988, went twenty-seven innings and droned on until nearly 4 A.M. With a chance to keep this one from going that far, Lewis hit a liner right back up the middle. Darwin snagged it and threw out Alomar for an inning-ending double play. The game marched on.

Not counting on the contest laboring on for hours into the cool spring evening, the Indians had given away thousands of team calendars that, by the fourteenth inning, fans began crafting into paper airplanes and firing around Cleveland Stadium. Dozens sailed out onto the field or got stuck in the netting behind home plate as the remaining spectators desperately searched for entertainment.

In the bottom of the fifteenth, with runners on first and third and two out, Lofton attempted to lay a drag bunt down the first-base line, catch the Red Sox completely off-guard, and with Lofton's speed probably win the game. But Lofton popped the bunt up into the air and a moment later the inning was over. The game marched on.

At about the same time Lofton's roll of the dice came up snake eyes, patrons visiting the concession stands at the Stadium discovered that their selection of nourishment had become decidedly slim. Almost everything was sold out. All that remained were peanuts and candy bars.

By the sixteenth, both bullpens were as tapped as a tailgate keg, and the teams were relying on their last resorts. Boston manager Butch Dobson took out Jeff Reardon in the sixteenth and inserted Mike Gardiner, who was supposed to start the first game of Sunday's doubleheader. Conversely, Hargrove replaced Steve Olin with Eric Bell in the fourteenth, and although he had Scott Scudder, a projected Sunday starter, warming up in the bullpen in the innings to follow, it was Bell or bust. Sunday's *Plain Dealer* recounted Hargrove's reply when asked postgame what it would have taken to get Scudder to the mound. "Eric Bell would have to die," he said.

As the Indians and Red Sox scurried to find pitching solutions on this most unorthodox opening day, back in Boston Roger Clemens returned from a late-afternoon jog and flipped on the television. He was set to pitch in the Red Sox home opener on Monday after getting treatment on his dislocated right little finger during the week. To his amazement, his team was still playing and was now into the seventeenth inning.

A few minutes later the phone rang in the Boston clubhouse at Cleveland Stadium. It was Clemens, calling to tell Dobson that he could pitch tomorrow if the manager needed him. It was like asking a politician if he'd like to do a television interview. Clemens's next call was to book a flight to Cleveland for early the next morning.

Meanwhile, the Indians and Red Sox toiled on into the crisp, falling dusk.

As the temperatures dropped into the forties, the Indians again appeared poised to end this ordeal in the bottom of the eighteenth. Rohde, who had been denied a chance to win the game in the thirteenth, drew a one-out walk, and Lofton did the same. After Hill struck out, Baerga hit a sharp grounder to Boston shortstop and Cincinnati native Tim Naehring, who managed to get in front of the ball but couldn't handle it, and everybody was safe. Had the ball scooted past Naehring, the ballgame would have been over. It was ruled Baerga's sixth hit of the game in his ninth at-bat, a truly remarkable performance, especially since he started the season by going 0-for-12 in Baltimore.

With Baerga at first and the winning run ninety feet from home, things didn't look good for Boston, especially when Albert Belle stepped to the plate. Proving that he still had a ways to go before he became one of the premier hitters in baseball, Belle struck out to end the inning, and, once again, the game marched on—but not for much longer.

Moments later the Red Sox started to ring Cleveland's other Bell as Vaughn drew a leadoff walk, then was bunted to second by Tony Pena, who went 0-for-7 on the day. Naehring, Boston's number nine hitter, worked the count to 2-and-2 on the tiring Bell before blasting a changeup out of the park just over Glenallen Hill's glove and inside the left-field foul pole for a 7-5 Boston lead. It was Naehring's first home run in two years.

A bystander at Cleveland Stadium in the moments that followed might have thought that Moses had appeared in the bleachers simultaneously with Naehring's home run, because the few thousand remaining fans poured toward the exits like Israelites heading back to their homeland.

But it wasn't over yet.

Sorrento doubled with one out in the bottom of the nineteenth, but Sandy Alomar was retired, leaving it all up to Rohde, who *would* get his chance to be the hero this time. Instead, at 8:13 P.M., after 19 innings, 586 pitches, 34 hits, 29 strikeouts, 16 walks, and 12 runs, Rohde grounded out to end the longest game in Cleveland history, exactly six-and-a-half hours after it had begun.

Although the loss was disappointing for the Indians, they really couldn't blame anyone but themselves. Sorrento became the eighteenth runner that Cleveland had stranded in the game, the tenth in extra innings.

When it was all over the Indians were 1-3, and their reward for losing a nineteen-inning game in the home opener was getting to play eighteen innings the next day and going up against their nemesis, Clemens, who held a 15-2 career record with a 2.24 ERA against the Indians.

Naturally Clemens worked his magic on Sunday, going the distance and defeating the Indians, 3-0, on two hits in the second game of the doubleheader. Still the Indians' offense actually did better against Clemens than in the first game. Boston's Matt Young pitched a no-hitter–but *lost,* 2-1, when Lofton walked and scored on an error and Lewis later walked and scored on a fielder's choice. The two hits off Clemens were the Indians' only safeties on Sunday, the fewest ever in a major-league doubleheader.

It had to be the craziest home-opening weekend in Indians' history. When the Red Sox left town Sunday night they and the Indians had played a grand total of thirty-seven innings in thirty hours. And there were still 156 games to go in the season.

Two years after that long opening day the Indians again found themselves trailing going into their sixth at-bat in the home opener, but this time they weren't just looking a tough loss in the face as they had against Boston in 1992. By the end of the sixth inning, believers in fate had already chalked up a no-hitter for Randy Johnson.

Any pitcher who has ever tossed a no-hitter will admit that a little bit of luck is needed to pull off one of the toughest tasks in the sport. There has to be perfect control and a few clutch plays on defense. And there has to be a controversial call or two that goes the pitcher's way.

Leading off the inning, Mark Lewis made the most impressive comeback of the afternoon thus far. He fell behind 0-and-2 after a fastball crossed the plate at his thighs, and he waved at a curveball in the dirt. After taking a high fastball Lewis checked his swing on a low curve for ball two. He took ball three checking his swing again and then received a free trip to first base when Johnson missed low and outside with a slider. It was Johnson's fourth walk of the afternoon and the first time an Indians' leadoff man had reached base since the first inning. Indians' fans buzzed a little bit, hoping this would be the inning they'd finally get to the six-foot-ten dominator. But those hopes came to a quick halt on the next pitch.

Kenny Lofton pounded a fastball into the dirt toward second, where Fermin snagged it going to his left and made a feeble attempt to tag Lewis, who maneuvered to his right while going into second. After feigning the tag on Lewis, Fermin threw on to Tino Martinez, beating Lofton by half a step. But second base umpire Al Clark called it a double play, saying that Lewis was out for running out of the baseline. As Lewis silently began jogging back to the dugout, the crowd realized what the call was and, for the first time ever at Jacobs Field, booed a contro-versial call.

Clark's decision brought Mike Hargrove out of the dugout and over to sec-ond base, where the two exchanged thoughts for several seconds before Hargrove returned to his seat, mumbling to himself.

Good call or not, the bases were now empty with two out and Omar Vizquel at bat. Vizquel popped Johnson's first pitch into foul territory along the third-base line, where Mike Blowers caught it to end the inning.

As the Mariners jogged in from the field the sellout crowd booed once again, and Chris Berman appropriately told his ESPN audience that it was the first time the crowd had made any notable noise for the entire game.

In the sixth, the Indians scored no runs on no hits, and there were no errors.

THE SEVENTH

	1	2	3	4	5	6	7	8	9			R	H	E
SEATTLE	1	0	1	0	0	0						2	3	1
CLEVELAND	0	0	0	0	0	0						0	0	1

Bob Feller (left) is all smiles as he gives an interview a day after throwing the only open-ing-day no-hitter in baseball history in 1940. That distinction would be seriously chal-lenged fifty-four years later. (*Cleveland Press* Collection, Cleveland State University)

Dennis Martinez missed high with a curveball to Rich Amaral to start the seventh, then came back with a pair of strikes: a curve right down the middle and another breaker that Amaral fouled down the first-base line. He sent Martinez's fourth pitch to the same place. After an inside fastball evened the count at 2-and-2, Martinez got Amaral to chase a low breaking ball, which Sandy Alomar dropped. Backing away from the plate after his swing, Amaral was almost tackled by Alomar going for the ball as he then lunged to tag the Seattle second baseman. As Amaral returned to the dugout, a victim of Martinez's third strikeout, Alomar and home plate umpire Larry Barnett joked about his potential prowess as a nose tackle.

Mike Blowers stepped in next and belted Martinez's 100th pitch of the afternoon into medium-deep center, where Kenny Lofton got a great jump and caught the ball on his hip directly behind second base.

With two out Ken Griffey Jr. was hoping to finally make an impact in what had been a frustrating afternoon. Following a walk in the first, he'd struck out in the third and then nubbed a ground out in the fifth. This time he went ahead 2-and-0 when a fastball sailed outside and a breaking ball dipped low. Martinez's third pitch caught the outside corner, but he then missed outside with another curve to fall behind 3-and-1. On the fifth pitch Griffey tapped a slow grounder down the third-base line that rolled foul twenty feet in front of the bag. On the sixth he did the same. Martinez then made Griffey look silly for the third straight at-bat by firing a perfect low breaking ball that Griffey swung at and missed for Martinez's fourth strikeout.

Martinez sprinted back to the dugout having retired nine of the last ten batters. Griffey would be the last batter he'd face, but Martinez had done everything Mike Hargrove could have asked: he kept his team in the game against one of baseball's top pitchers. It was a role he would become accustomed to in the future, and he'd play it to perfection during the biggest victory of his career eighteen months later.

In the seventh, the Mariners scored no runs on no hits, and there were no errors.

	1	2	3	4	5	6	7	8	9			R	H	E
SEATTLE	1	0	1	0	0	0	0					2	3	1
CLEVELAND	0	0	0	0	0	0						0	0	1

Later that afternoon Sandy Alomar described to the *Akron Beacon Journal* what he felt was one of the most memorable moments the day. When the suddenly energetic Martinez reached the dugout he gave his teammates a quick pep talk. "It's the seventh inning and this guy is throwing a no-no!" he yelled. "So let's do something!"

It was as if Martinez, along with everyone else in the ballpark, was slowly beginning to realize that they could be in for a little more history than they'd bargained for. Randy Johnson was just three innings away from being immortalized as the second major-league pitcher ever to throw a no-hitter on opening day.

In case the Indians needed any more motivation to break up Johnson's goose egg, the only other opening-day no-hitter had been one of the great moments in their franchise's history. If they were unable to slap one through the infield in the next three innings, Cleveland's most famous pitcher would have to surrender one of his few remaining records.

For twenty-one-year-old Bob Feller, April 16, 1940, didn't seem like a day he'd remember for the rest of his life. He was entering his fifth season with the Indians and coming off an impressive 1939 campaign in which he won twenty-four games with a 2.85 ERA. On this first opening day of the decade, he was set to face the White Sox at Comiskey Park on a damp forty-seven-degree day with a nasty breeze coming in off Lake Michigan.

It was a miserable day for baseball, but for Feller's mother, who was in attendance with his father and sister (and nearly fourteen thousand others), it was bound to be better than her last trip to Comiskey. The previous Mother's Day, Feller had acquired seats along the first-base line for his parents and sister to see him pitch against the White Sox. It had been a wonderful afternoon for Mrs. Feller until Chicago third baseman Marv Owen hit a line-drive foul into the seats that hit her squarely in the face. She left the game immediately and spent the next two weeks in the hospital with two black eyes and a badly scratched face.

While his mother was showing a lot of courage by returning to the site of a painful memory, Feller himself was out to rinse a bad taste from his mouth. He was coming off a sub-par performance in his final exhibition game against the

New York Giants, when he was tapped for fifteen hits and ten runs in five innings. No one expected Feller to break any records this opening day, particularly when he didn't look sharp early.

In the second inning Chicago right fielder Taft Wright reached base on an error when Indians' center fielder Roy Weatherly misplayed a fly ball. Feller compounded the problem by walking the next two batters, but a strikeout of Bob Kennedy got him out of trouble. At that point, Feller decided to abandon his curveball, since it was too damp and chilly to control it completely. For the final seven innings he threw only fastballs and found a rhythm that carried him through.

As Feller heated up, the Indians' offense was having just as much trouble as Chicago's was. White Sox starter Edgar Smith, who had defeated Feller 1-0 in Chicago the previous August, was almost as good as Feller, going eight innings, striking out five batters, and allowing just six hits.

But a pair of those hits decided the game. Jeff Heath, Feller's road roommate, singled in the fourth and scored on catcher Rollie Hemsley's triple to right center. It would be the only run of the game, but as the contest drew toward its conclusion the final score wasn't what everyone was interested in. They wanted to see if Bob Feller could do what no one had ever done before—throw a no-hitter on opening day.

At one point during the game a photographer snuck onto the dugout steps and crouched to snap a picture of Feller sitting on the bench, but he was denied by Feller's conscientious teammates. It was a theme that persevered as the afternoon wore on. Feller sat alone in the dugout between innings, since nobody wanted to jinx what he had going. In the seventh inning Heath couldn't stand the tension anymore and walked over to his roomie, as the *Plain Dealer* recounted:

"Well, Robert . . ." he began.

"Another word," snarled pitcher Harry Eisenstat, "and I'll stick my hand down your throat to the elbow."

Heath quietly sat down.

According to the *Plain Dealer*, the only words anyone heard Feller mutter during the course of the game came a few moments later when his sacrifice bunt attempt ended up forcing Ray Mack at third. Feller mumbled, "That was a lousy bunt," as he picked up his glove back at the bench.

After dodging a bullet in the eighth when second baseman Mack made a great play on a Larry Rosenthal grounder, Feller finally reached the ninth, three outs away from the history books.

The first batter he faced was center fielder Mike Kreevich, who went ahead 2-and-0 before Feller came back with a strike and then forced a foul to even the count. Kreevich popped up the fifth toss onto the right side of the infield, where Mack caught it. Two outs away.

When Julius "Moose" Solters stepped to the plate next, Feller had to do more than just retire another batter—he also had to prevent history from repeating itself.

Solters was a former Indian, and three times in the previous two years Feller had been denied a no-hitter by former Tribesmen. On April 20, 1938, Billy Sullivan of the St. Louis Browns broke up a no-no by beating out a bunt, as did Boston's Bobby Doerr with a single on May 25, 1939. A month later on June 27 Earl Averill of the Tigers prevented Feller from pitching a no-hitter in the first-ever night game at Cleveland Stadium by picking up a single. Now Feller was hoping the fourth time was the charm.

Solters spanked Feller's third pitch toward short, but Lou Boudreau made an incredible stop and threw out his former teammate. One out away.

But the next White Sox batter was shortstop Luke Appling, a man notorious to American League pitchers and one of the toughest outs in the game. Appling, who had once fouled off eighteen straight balls as a financial protest because he was upset with management over his contract, negotiated to 2-and-2 with Feller before going to work. He fouled off four straight pitches trying to tire out the hard-throwing righty, and Feller realized this was a battle he could ill-afford to lose. He opted to walk Appling "intentionally" by hurling a pair outside, sending him to first as a result of Feller's fourth walk of the game. Appling became Chicago's first baserunner since the third inning after Feller had retired twenty consecutive batters.

Feller's strategy brought up his longtime nemesis, right fielder Taft Wright, who had given him fits with the Washington Senators the previous two seasons and played an instrumental role in three Feller losses.

Feller missed with his first toss. Wright smoked his second offering on the ground toward right field, the hardest-hit ball off Feller all afternoon. But Mack came out of nowhere, diving to his left to knock it down with his glove. The ball skipped onto the rim of the outfield grass as Wright sprinted down the line toward first. Mack scrambled after it, scooped it up, and whirled it toward Hal Trosky at first. His throw beat Wright by a half a step.

Feller had done it.

After several near misses he had finally pitched a no-hitter, the first in the major leagues since Monte Pearson of the Yankees had done it against the Indians two seasons beforehand. It was the eighth time it had been done in Cleveland baseball history and the Indians' first since Wes Ferrell's gem over St. Louis on August 29, 1931. More important, Feller was the first ever to do it on opening day.

The Indians' locker room was naturally swarming with reporters and photographers after the game. One photographer asked Cleveland manager Oscar Vitt to pose with his arms around Feller. "You're darned right I'll hug him!" Vitt replied. "What a kid!"

Asked if he was excited on the mound as the no-hitter progressed, Feller told the *Plain Dealer*, "Well, I didn't have any trouble keepin' awake."

Despite some narrow escapes, the *Cleveland Press* called it "one of the most clean-cut no-hitters ever pitched, with no doubtful plays."

But the final out of the game might have been debated for years to come had Wright been a half-step faster. Ed Burns, a longtime Chicago sportswriter and the game's official scorer, said he would have ruled the play an error, which would have preserved the no-hitter. Feller disagreed.

"If Wright had reached first base," he told the *Press*, "I would have scored it as a hit myself. That ball was hard-hit."

The *Press* also noted Hemsley's good-natured reaction. Although he would have garnered praise for driving in the game's lone run, Hemsley couldn't help but sass Feller for receiving all the media attention.

"That's right, Feller, take those headlines away from me," he razzed. "He would pick today to pitch a no-hit game. I was all set to be the hero . . . Now nobody'll know I was in the contest."

Once the locker room cleared, Feller left the ballpark for a quiet dinner with his parents and sister, requesting that all reporters and photographers leave him alone for the occasion.

It was almost an incredibly historic day for baseball as word trickled into Chicago that Boston's Lefty Grove, who'd shut the Indians down in the first-ever game at Cleveland Stadium, also had a no-hitter going in the nation's capital against the Senators. With President Roosevelt in attendance, Grove took his date with destiny into the eighth inning before Washington's Cecil Travis broke it up with a single. The Red Sox, just like the Indians, won, 1-0.

Cleveland fans understood how special an achievement Feller's opening-day no-hitter was. When the Indians returned to Cleveland two days later for a series with the Tigers, seven thousand fans greeted them (or maybe just Feller) at Union Terminal downtown. Some remarked that they hadn't seen anything like it since the Indians won the 1920 World Series.

They'd enjoy the feeling again during Feller's career, as he threw two more no-hitters: against the Yankees in 1946 and against the Tigers in 1951. Despite missing three seasons while he served in the United States Navy during World War II (he was the first professional athlete to enlist following the bombing of Pearl Harbor) he retired in 1956 with 266 victories, all with the Indians, and a 3.25 career ERA. His number 19 was retired by the Indians in 1957 (and re-retired on opening day 1994), and he was inducted into the Baseball Hall of Fame in 1962.

For more than five decades no one had really threatened Feller's place in history. Now the seventy-five-year-old hall-of-famer was getting a little squeamish in his seat at Jacobs Field as Randy Johnson drew closer to forever linking their names in the record books. With the heart of Cleveland's order coming to bat in the bottom of the seventh, many felt that this would be the club's last legitimate shot to get back into the game—or simply just get a hit.

Carlos Baerga took a fastball down the middle for strike one to lead off the Indians' half of the seventh. He then attempted to bunt a Johnson slider, and the result was a high-pop foul to the left of home plate. Dan Wilson sprinted after it, but the ball landed six feet in front of him. Down 0-and-2, Baerga took a fastball low for ball one and then took a seat after what might have been Johnson's best pitch of the day. Knowing that Baerga was expecting a fastball, Johnson painted the outside corner of the plate perfectly with a breaking ball that froze the Tribe's second baseman and made him Johnson's second strikeout victim.

Albert Belle stepped into the box and went ahead of Johnson 2-and-0. Belle chopped Johnson's third pitch foul down the third-base line for strike one, then took another heater low for ball three. On the fifth pitch destiny once again appeared to be on Randy Johnson's side.

Belle ripped a low fastball into deep center field, and Griffey gave chase. The crowd roared at the crack of the bat but began to groan as Griffey slowed down on the warning track near the junction of the nineteen-foot left-field wall and the eight-foot center-field wall. He caught Belle's blast in that nook 404 feet from home plate, six feet short of the wall in the deepest part of the ballpark. If the ball had been ten feet to the right or left, it would have been off the wall or possibly over it. Wishful thinking aside, it was simply out number two. Eddie Murray stepped up next.

The crack of the bat sounded exactly like on the previous pitch, as Murray tattooed Johnson's first offering right back to center. This one was hit neither as hard nor as high as Belle's, and Griffey barely had to move to catch the line drive in the middle of the outfield for the third out.

With the meat of the Cleveland lineup now retired for possibly the final time, Randy Johnson was just six outs away from the first opening-day no-hitter in fifty-four years.

Bob Feller's discomfort level was rising by the moment.

In the seventh, the Indians scored no runs on no hits, and there were no errors.

THE EIGHTH

	1	2	3	4	5	6	7	8	9			R	H	E
SEATTLE	1	0	1	0	0	0	0					2	3	1
CLEVELAND	0	0	0	0	0	0	0					0	0	1

Seattle's Randy Johnson had a no-hitter going into the eighth inning. (*Akron Beacon Journal*)

As the Indians and Mariners traded places in the field, "King of Wishful Thinking" by Go West played over the speakers at Jacobs Field, perhaps summing up the mindset of the Indians going into the final two innings.

But before they could get another shot to interrupt Randy Johnson's date with history, they had to get through the top of the eighth, and they'd be doing it with a new face on the mound.

Replacing Dennis Martinez was former Mariner Russ Swan, a lefty the Indians had signed as a free agent in January. After joining Seattle in 1990 Swan's ERA had skyrocketed over the course of three seasons. From 3.43 in 1991, it jumped to 4.74 in 1992, and then to a disturbing 9.15 in twenty-three games in 1993. Looking for a fresh start in Cleveland, Swan would start the eighth as the first relief pitcher to make an appearance at Jacobs Field.

Meanwhile Dennis Martinez stayed in the Cleveland dugout with a warm-up jacket on and a towel around his neck. Just his presence in the dugout, when most veteran pitchers would have retired to the clubhouse, meant a lot to his teammates. It seemed to signal a new era not only for the Indians' pitching staff but also for the entire organization.

"It says something about a guy who stays on the bench the whole game and roots for the guys," Sandy Alomar later told the *Beacon Journal*. "He didn't have to do that."

Swan fooled Jay Buhner into a swing and a miss on a curve, then missed first with a curveball in the dirt and then with a high fastball. Buhner nubbed Swan's fourth pitch toward second, where Carlos Baerga charged, barehanded the ball, and tossed it to Eddie Murray for the first out.

Eric Anthony stepped into the box next, and it seemed like weeks since he had driven in the game's only two runs. He cut at and missed the ball on a sharp slider, then popped a slow curve to short center field, where Baerga caught it on the grass just to the left of second base.

Tino Martinez would now attempt to keep this from becoming the second consecutive one-two-three inning for the visitors. He took ball one on a curve in the dirt, then watched a breaking ball pinch the inside corner to even the count. On the third toss he broke his bat on a slider, and the ball floated over the infield and dropped into center for the fourth Seattle hit.

Keeping an eye on Martinez at first Swan rebounded with a fastball down the middle to jump ahead of Reggie Jefferson, then missed outside with a curve. He came back with two straight breaking balls that Jefferson swung at and missed to end the inning.

Swan jogged back to the dugout having done his job, but it would not be a good spring or summer for the southpaw. In seven more appearances with Cleveland, Swan would surrender ten runs, plus lose a wild 12-9 game to Kansas City in relief twelve days after the opener. He was sent to AAA Charlotte on May 1 and finished his season there with a 1-3 record and a 7.09 ERA. He never again pitched in the major leagues.

In the eighth, the Mariners scored no runs on one hit, and there were no errors.

	1	2	3	4	5	6	7	8	9			R	H	E
SEATTLE	1	0	1	0	0	0	0					2	4	1
CLEVELAND	0	0	0	0	0	0						0	0	1

As Randy Johnson walked to the mound for the bottom of the eighth inning, longtime Cleveland fans had to be glumly thinking that this whole scenario seemed appropriate.

This beautiful new ballpark and new batch of talented players represented years of planning, building, and hoping for a new birth for the Indians. This day was supposed to restitute the franchise's previous shortcomings. Instead, everything was going to be shattered like a broken mirror by the tallest player ever to play the game of baseball.

A no-hitter against the Indians on opening day would be offensive for several reasons. It would be baseball's first since Bob Feller had done it in 1940 and thus would unseat him as the sole owner of a prestigious historical distinction. Second, it would prove to many that the Indians simply could not avoid bad luck, regardless of where they played. While a no-hitter would be nowhere near as tragic as the shroud that had hung over the team's opener the year before, it would continue a trend of crushing any springtime hopes in Cleveland before they even started. Finally, no one would ever forget that in the Indians' first game in their brand new ballpark they were victims of a no-hitter.

Although it would be impulsive to put too much emphasis on one game in a sport that includes 162 in the regular season, the ramifications of a no-hitter there and then—especially for a team with as fragile a past as the Indians—can't be overstated. If the Indians were unable to come up with a hit in these final two innings, many assumed, it could cripple the team in the first few weeks of the season, particularly at home. Crowds would probably go to the park for all of its inaugural season—and possibly for years thereafter—thinking there was no true home-field advantage. A team that gets no-hit in its first game in a new ballpark must feel as though it's been cheated with the utmost cruelty.

The Chicago White Sox demonstrated this principle when they opened the new Comiskey Park in 1991. They were buried 16-0 by the Detroit Tigers that day, and aside from the 1993 divisional champion team, Comiskey didn't provide much of a home-field advantage for the remainder of the decade. Obviously other factors were involved, but the tone set on a sunny April afternoon in Chicago seemed to last at least for the remainder of the season and beyond. If the Indians didn't act soon Jacobs Field might become a $169 million lemon, simply a much nicer venue as the home of the same old Indians.

As the Indians' odds were growing longer right along with the late-afternoon shadows, Candy Maldonado stepped into the box and did his best to keep Johnson out of the record books. After going around on a check swing on a first-pitch curveball, Maldonado took four straight balls—a breaking ball low and a trio of fastballs: outside, high, then outside again. As Maldonado jogged to first, the beneficiary of Johnson's fifth walk, Johnson rolled his eyes and head simultaneously, swearing to himself.

Paralleling that sentiment, the Mariners were discovering a minor kink in the plush confines of Jacobs Field: the phone from their dugout to the bullpen didn't work. From the dugout steps pitching coach Sammy Ellis motioned out to the right-field bullpen, and moments later lefty Tim Davis began warming up.

Johnson uncorked his 100th pitch, a fastball strike that grazed the outside corner to Sandy Alomar. Johnson then missed low with a breaking ball but struck back with a similar pitch that nipped the outside corner. Alomar turned to Larry Barnett with a "You-just-called-that-a-ball" look. Although down 1-and-2 Alomar quickly forgot about it and focused on Johnson's fourth pitch, a fastball. He swung.

Swung on, lined through the right side, a base hit! Herb Score told his radio audience.

Alomar clubbed the ball through the hole between first and second and into right field for the Indians' first hit of the game, of the season, and in their new ballpark.

Stopping at second base, Candy Maldonado. There is the first hit in Jacobs Field for an Indian. Sandy Alomar has it, and the Indians with runners at first and at second and nobody out here in the eighth inning. For the first time this afternoon, this big crowd has something to cheer for for the Indians.

A sudden whoosh of breeze gusted through Jacobs Field, but it didn't come off Lake Erie. It was 41,459 simultaneous sighs of relief. Alomar, with his first hit in eleven career at-bats against Johnson, seemed energized and pounded his hands together at first.

As Maldonado reached second, Buhner fired the ball back in, and the capacity crowd was going bonkers. They'd been waiting all day for something to get excited about, and appropriately, one of the players who had been with the Indians the longest—through four very long, very poor seasons—had provided the hometown team with its first hit at Jacobs Field.

"I wasn't thinking about it being the first hit," Alomar later told reporters. "I needed to put the ball in play, and I was just fortunate that it found a hole. . . . Candy helped me by walking. They were holding him on first, and that gave me a hole to shoot for."

The truly conscientious could only wonder: might Bob Feller's presence have had something to do with the breakup? "If Johnson's superstitious," Feller later said to the *Plain Dealer*, "he'll hate me for the rest of his life."

Even though he'd gone on to set several other records, pitch in two World Series, and be inducted into the Baseball Hall of Fame, Feller was very clearly proud of his unique accomplishment and was rooting for the Indians to get a hit so that he could hang onto it.

"I was concerned," Feller told the *Plain Dealer*. "I've sweated it out for fifty-some years. It's about the only (record) I've got left except the most bases on balls (208) in one year (1938). That's one Nolan Ryan didn't get from me."

As the ball was returned to Johnson and Manny Ramirez walked toward the batter's box, the "charge" cry was played over the speakers for the first time ever in a regular-season game at Jacobs Field.

Obviously flustered, Johnson fired his next pitch over Wilson's head and to the backstop, giving the now-rambunctious crowd more fuel for its fire. Maldonado advanced to third and Alomar to second.

Less than five minutes earlier, the Indians had all but abandoned any hopes of scoring, let alone winning. The quest for the remaining two innings had been to hit a ball somewhere—*any*where—to prevent a cloud of bad karma from settling over Jacobs Field. All of a sudden the tying runs were in scoring position with no outs, and the crowd was rocking.

Even better news for the Indians was that Ramirez would not have to bunt, as he was instructed to do by Mike Hargrove. He had been squared to try to advance the runners when Johnson did it himself by trying to toss the ball up to Bob Feller. Now Hargrove could let the twenty-one-year old rookie take a few swings and see what he could do against a now-vulnerable Johnson.

It only took one.

Manny Ramirez steps in, ball one . . . Score said.

Ramirez blasted Johnson's next pitch, a fastball down and in and right in his wheelhouse.

long drive! left field! way back . . .

The ball sailed into the outfield, seemingly carried by the roar of the crowd, which was now finally experiencing some of the timeless excitement of opening day.

it's back . . . it's going . . . it's off the wall!

It hit the nineteen-foot wall twelve feet up and bounced back down onto the grass to the left of Eric Anthony, who was turned the other way and had to scamper after it.

Two runs will score! Into second base is Ramirez with a double!

While Maldonado scored and Alomar rounded third and headed for home, Ramirez coasted into second with the first Cleveland RBIs at Jacobs Field on the second double of his career. Alomar crossed the plate as Anthony tossed the ball to Felix Fermin covering third, and the sellout crowd was on its feet and reveling in the start of something captivating.

And listen to this crowd! The Indians have tied it here in the eighth!

As Ramirez's shot bounced off the wall, Johnson closed his eyes in frustration and slowly marched to the plate to back up Wilson. For the first time in the afternoon, a walk had come back to hurt him, and not only was his bid for a no-hitter out the window, but with the go-ahead run at second and no outs, his bid for a victory was in jeopardy as well.

But just as it had been earlier, good fortune remained on Johnson's side. On the next pitch he missed high to Mark Lewis with a fastball, but as Wilson received it he noticed the Cleveland rookie right fielder wandering a bit far off of second base. He rifled the baseball to Fermin moving toward second as Ramirez stumbled trying to get back six feet from the bag. Fermin caught Wilson's toss and tagged a head-first sliding Ramirez a foot in front of second base for the huge first out. Still the crowd gave Ramirez a hearty round of applause as he trotted back to the dugout.

With the bleeding now stopped, Johnson could focus solely on Lewis, who fouled off a fastball, a slider, and a curve to go down 1-and-2. He tapped Johnson's fifth offering back toward the mound, where Johnson snagged it, jogged toward first, and flipped it to Tino Martinez for the second out.

Kenny Lofton would now try to salvage the opportunity as he fell down 0-and-1 on a fastball. The count evened as a slider bit inside on a Lofton bunt attempt, and the former Arizona Wildcat went ahead 2-and-1 when a curve sent him spinning like a top out of the box. Lofton popped the fourth pitch off the handle of the bat and into left field, where Eric Anthony snagged it in the growing shadows of the toothbrush lights to retire the side.

But the Indians had rescued the entire day. Regardless of what happened from this point on, Sandy Alomar had kept inhumane irony out of downtown Cleveland, and Manny Ramirez had brought the concept of poetic justice back in. Even more satisfying for the Indians was that a rookie the team had invested so much in three years earlier had just christened the franchise's new palace by knocking in its first runs to tie the game on opening day. Things were starting to get good.

The time for looking back was over. The future was at hand.

In the eighth, the Indians scored two runs on two hits, and there were no errors.

THE NINTH

	1	2	3	4	5	6	7	8	9				R	H	E
SEATTLE	1	0	1	0	0	0	0	0					2	4	1
CLEVELAND	0	0	0	0	0	0	0	2					2	2	1

Catcher Sandy Alomar Jr. (back) celebrates with designated hitter Candy Maldonado after scoring the Indians' first-ever runs at Jacobs Field in the eighth inning. (*Akron Beacon Journal*)

If Manny Ramirez's at-bat seemed Hollywoodesque to Cleveland fans, still buzzing as the Indians took the field for the ninth, there was a legitimate reason. More than just YOUNGSTER COMES UP BIG ON OPENING DAY IN NEW PARK, his clutch double appeared to be straight out of a screenplay.

In the 1989 comedy *Major League,* which portrayed the Indians transforming from a group of has-beens and never-will-bes to pennant-contenders, Cleveland trailed 2-0 going into the bottom of the seventh inning in its one-game playoff with the New York Yankees for the AL East championship. Following a two-out single by third baseman Roger Dorn (played by Corbin Bernsen), right fielder Pedro Cerrano (played by Dennis Haysbert) stepped up to pound a game-tying home run off the league's best pitcher over the left-field fence and out of Cleveland Stadium. The game went into the ninth inning tied at two before Ricky "Wild Thing" Vaughn (Charlie Sheen) shut down the Yankees in the top of the inning, and Jake Taylor (Tom Berenger) beat out a bunt to score Willie "Mays" Hayes (Wesley Snipes) and win the division. The film's ill-fated sequel was just released the week before Jacobs Field opened.

In case Ramirez's double wasn't enough of an allusion for a five-minute period, as the Indians took the field in the ninth they had a brand-new pitcher in what had become a brand-new ballgame. In the near future, Jose Mesa taking the mound for the Indians in the ninth inning would seem as natural as heading for second base after rounding first. However, as he warmed up in the waning afternoon sunlight, Mesa readied to pitch in relief for just the fourth time.

Mesa's major-league career had begun the same way as many of the Latin American players' who had preceded him. Born and raised in a tiny town in the Dominican Republic in a family of twenty-five children, Mesa was offered a contract by the Toronto Blue Jays in October 1981 when he was just fifteen years old. He spent six years in the Toronto farm system but never rose above the AA level before being traded to Baltimore in 1987. He made his major-league debut with the Orioles that September and made five starts with limited success before spending the next two seasons in the minors rehabilitating from two elbow surgeries. After a great finish with Baltimore in 1990 elbow problems again forced him back to the minors a year later, although he managed to win six games for the Orioles.

After a rocky start in 1992 Mesa was shipped to the Indians in July for a minor-league outfielder named Kyle Washington and was immediately inserted into the starting rotation despite his unimpressive 13-24 career record with Baltimore. Mesa was a nice surprise for the Tribe in the second half of the season, going 4-4 with a 4.16 ERA on a team that needed pitching the way New York City needs traffic lights. What's more, Cleveland was 10-5 in games Mesa started. He earned a dubious distinction in the record books on September 9 in Milwaukee when he gave up Robin Yount's 3,000th career hit, but five days later he outdueled Toronto's David Cone in a 2-1 Indians' win. It was clear that Mesa would be a part of the Indians' future pitching plans.

Mesa led the team in victories, innings pitched, and strikeouts in 1993, including three complete games and with a 4.92 ERA. On May 9 Mesa made the third relief appearance of his career and the first with Cleveland when he held the White Sox hitless for an inning. Although he never came out of the bullpen for the remainder of the season, it was a preview of coming attractions for the twenty-six-year-old fireballer.

To help shore up a monstrously weak bullpen in 1994 pitching coach Phil Regan talked Mesa into becoming a reliever. Mesa wasn't crazy about the idea at first, since he figured leaving the starting rotation for the bullpen was the first step toward oblivion. But John Hart and Mike Hargrove were hoping Mesa's brute strength and fabulous fastball could eventually propel him into the role of Cleveland's closer. Free-agent acquisition Steve Farr held that job to start the 1994 season, but it wasn't set in stone and, as it turned out, didn't work. In spring training a year later the Indians would find themselves asking the same closer questions.

To kick off his 1994 season, Mesa uncorked his bread-and-butter, a 92-mph fastball that Dan Wilson fouled into the first-base seats for strike one. After missing high with another fastball, Wilson pounded another foul off Larry Barnett's chest protector and then hit a curve foul into the first-base seats again. After a fastball tailed inside, Wilson poked one into the same seats a third time before Mesa blew another fastball past his bat for strike three. Wilson flipped the bat up into the air and caught it with his left hand as he marched back to the dugout.

Mesa fired a fastball down the pike to Felix Fermin for strike one, then missed low with a curve to even the count. Fermin hit the next fastball toward the gap in right center. Both Lofton and Ramirez converged on it, and Ramirez almost made his second rookie mistake in five minutes.

With Lofton calling him off and waving his left hand in the air to signal that he was going to catch it, Ramirez kept coming, which forced the alert Lofton to slow down an instant before catching the ball. Lofton got his glove out in time and snagged the ball as Ramirez ran behind him. The pair had come within a foot of colliding. As they moved back to their respective positions, Lofton told the young prospect he had to listen for him on plays like that, motioning to his ear.

With two down, Rich Amaral stepped in and fouled a high fastball into the first-base seats, whose occupants were seeing a lot of action this inning. After taking another fastball low and outside, Amaral then took advantage of an earlier episode, revealing the game of baseball as the chess match that it is.

Recalling Amaral's two-out bunt attempt in the fourth, Indians' third baseman Mark Lewis was playing closer to the plate than he had in any of Amaral's previous appearances. On the third pitch, Amaral slapped a fastball straight down the third-base line, where it took an odd bounce, just eluding a diving Lewis, and sailed over the bag and into left field. Third-base umpire Dan Morrison was in perfect position and correctly called it a fair ball. Amaral motored into second as Albert Belle fielded it and threw it back to the infield.

Lewis peeled himself off the grass in foul territory knowing that he had been duped. Had he been playing Amaral as he had for every other at-bat, he would have had a much better chance to snag the ball. Adding to Lewis's problem was the growing shadow factor along the left side of the infield. With the sun beginning to set behind that side of Jacobs Field, the shadows of the light fixtures were gradually stretching longer across the infield. As the ball left Amaral's bat it went through two patches of sun and two patches of shade before it reached Lewis. It was just one of those quirks players discover in a new ballpark on opening day. The Mariners now had a chance to take back the lead with Mike Blowers up and Ken Griffey Jr. on deck.

Knowing that Mesa was still adjusting to his reliever role, both Sandy Alomar and Omar Vizquel headed to the mound to make sure everyone's signals were straight for Blowers in an at-bat that held crucial importance.

Mesa missed low and outside with a curve and then high with a fastball, and the crowd began to get a bit restless. The Indians had come too far to blow this thing in the ninth. Mesa, seeming to respond, got Blowers to tap a fastball lightly to third, where Lewis gathered it up and threw on to Eddie Murray for the third out.

Mesa's first ninth-inning relief appearance with the Indians resulted in a goose egg, a prelude for many more to come.

In the ninth, the Mariners scored no runs on one hit, and there were no errors.

	1	2	3	4	5	6	7	8	9			R	H	E
SEATTLE	1	0	1	0	0	0	0	0	0			2	5	1
CLEVELAND	0	0	0	0	0	0	0	2				2	2	1

The crowd crackled with excitement as the Indians jogged off the field. With the second, third, and fourth hitters in the Cleveland lineup coming up, the fans began to anticipate the drama of a possible win in the Tribe's last at-bat in the ninth inning to baptize their new yard. That possibility seemed a little more likely as they learned that Randy Johnson had been replaced by twenty-three-year-old left-hander Tim Davis, who was making his major-league debut.

Johnson sat at the end of the Seattle dugout, staring out at the field, perhaps trying to envision what might have been. As Davis finished his warmup tosses, Johnson stood up and skulked across the dugout to the stairway that led to the clubhouse. Instead of taking the mound in a vie for history, Johnson was hitting the showers while the Mariners' hopes of winning now rested on the arm of a rookie submariner.

Even though few Indians' fans would have mentioned it at the time, as Davis fired the first sidearm pitch of his career it looked like a familiar delivery from a recent member of the Cleveland bullpen—the late Steve Olin.

Omar Vizquel took that pitch, a curve for a strike, after feigning a bunt attempt. He then took another curve outside and a fastball high and inside to go ahead 2-and-1. On Davis' fourth pitch Vizquel popped a curve into foul territory a few feet along the first-base line. Frustrated with himself Vizquel jogged a few steps out of the box down the line still holding the bat and keeping his eye on the ball. Dan Wilson threw his mask off and moved to his right, as it appeared that he would be the one making the play. Just like Vizquel, Tino Martinez started moving down the first-base line in the opposite direction with his full attention on the ball.

As the trio converged, all three noticed that the ball was shifting direction and moving farther up along the line as it came down. Martinez started to make a quick move to catch it and then collided with Vizquel, who didn't see him, and fell to the ground along with the ball in foul territory. Barnett correctly called Vizquel out for interference, but Martinez lay curled up in the grass as Lou Piniella came out to check on his downed first baseman. He'd already lost one Martinez to injury today and didn't want to give up another.

The infield gathered around Martinez as he recovered from having the wind knocked out of him. A few seconds later he got up and jogged back to first as the crowd gave him a classy round of applause.

Davis returned to the mound and missed twice to Carlos Baerga with a pair of curveballs. Baerga smacked a third-pitch slider foul along the third-base line, then went ahead 3-and-1 when another slider drifted high. Baerga chopped the fifth toss slowly toward short, where Fermin glided in, gloved it, and fired on to first to get Baerga by a step.

As Albert Belle slowly marched from the on-deck circle to the batter's box, three shirtless young men sitting in the top row of the bleachers in left field rose to their feet and pointed hysterically to a sign they had made and tied to the metal grating behind them. A red target had been painted on it, along with the words "Hey, Albert!" Though their sign politely requested an opening-day souvenir in the form of a home run baseball, this trio wasn't picky. Anywhere Belle wanted to aim the ball over the fence right now would be fine by them.

He came close on Davis' first offering, a curve that Belle barely missed crushing and fouled back into the first-base seats. The crowd "ooh"-ed, knowing that the left fielder had the rookie's timing down cold. Davis missed with a slider outside then came back with another curveball that Belle rocketed fair down the first-base line over Martinez's head and into right field. As Belle rounded first and the ball bounced into the cranny between a pocket of stands and the right-field corner, a fan reached out and snagged the ball. First-base umpire Greg Kosc quickly called fan interference, granting Belle a ground-rule double. Belle wasn't going any farther than second anyway, and now with Eddie Murray stepping up the Indians had a chance to win a game they were only hoping not to end hitless less than a half-hour before.

The crowd began to chant, "Ed-die! Ed-die!"

On Davis's first pitch Murray ripped a curve down the left-field line and into the outfield, where it landed less than three feet foul on the rubberized track. Belle was halfway between third and home when he stopped and slowly started jogging back to second. For 2½ seconds the sellout crowd sounded like a tornado, then groaned with the realization that instead of claiming victory all Murray had done was collect strike one. As he stepped back in the "charge" theme was played for the second time that afternoon.

The thirty-eight-year-old stretched and missed at a changeup way outside of the strike zone to go down 0-and-2, and it appeared that Davis was about to get out of the inning. He tried to dip into that well a second time, but Murray didn't chase and stayed alive. He checked his swing on the fourth pitch, an offspeeder, but made contact and couldn't have placed it any better. It rolled onto the grass between third and home, just far enough away from Wilson, Davis, and Mike Blowers to allow Murray to reach first with a single and Belle to make it to third. Although it was not exactly the kind of hit he'd been known for throughout his career, it was Murray's first as an Indian.

With righty Bobby Ayala making ready in the Seattle bullpen and Candy Maldonado on deck, Lou Piniella motioned to Wilson to go to the mound to talk to Davis and give Ayala a few more seconds to warm up. After a brief discussion, Piniella made the march out to the mound himself and motioned for Ayala.

In a bullpen with just about as many question marks as were in Cleveland's, Ayala was slated to be Seattle's closer. Hoping Bobby Thigpen could return to his ace reliever form (which he'd played with the Chicago White Sox from 1988 to 1991), the Mariners had picked him up as a free-agent experiment from Philadelphia in the offseason. Just a few days before spring training closed, they'd also acquired the ageless Goose Gossage, who'd spent the last two of his twenty-two major-league seasons in Oakland. Both would make minor contributions to the Mariners in 1994, which would also be their last season.

After spending two sub-par years in Cincinnati, one with Piniella at the helm, Ayala came to the Mariners in a trade for Bret Boone and Erik Hanson. He now had the task of getting his new team into extra innings in his first appearance.

Naturally, Mike Hargrove didn't want righty Maldonado facing righty Ayala with the game on the line, so he pulled back the Candy Man for power-hitting lefty Paul Sorrento. Sorrento would be the team's everyday starting first baseman whenever the Tribe wasn't facing a left-hander the caliber of Randy Johnson. Though he'd hit just .257 in 1993, he'd blasted eighteen home runs, knocked in sixty-five RBI, and proved to be a valuable asset to a team with little power apart from Albert Belle. Now Sorrento had a chance to kick off the new season with style.

He tried to check his swing on Ayala's first offering, an offspeed toss that dipped low, but he went too far, and Barnett rang it up as strike one. He successfully checked his swing on the next pitch, a splitfingered fastball that sank low to even the count. After another offspeed pitch sailed outside, Sorrento again went too far on a check swing on an inside changeup. Eddie Murray moved to second with no effort by Seattle to throw him out.

Before Ayala could uncork the next toss Sorrento called time and stepped out of the box. Fermin jogged over to the mound to talk briefly with his pitcher, then back to his position.

Ayala's fifth pitch fooled Sorrento completely. It was a magnificent changeup that sank out of the strike zone. Sorrento, looking for something higher, cut and missed to end the inning, stranding two runners in scoring position. Ayala had done the job and begun what would be a sparkling season.

It was only appropriate after five long years of planning and preparation for this afternoon that the first-ever game in Cleveland's first baseball-only ballpark would go a little longer than expected.

In the ninth, the Indians scored no runs on two hits, and there were no errors.

THE TENTH

	1	2	3	4	5	6	7	8	9	10			R	H	E
SEATTLE	1	0	1	0	0	0	0	0	0				2	5	1
CLEVELAND	0	0	0	0	0	0	0	2	0				2	4	1

Perhaps the most telling play of opening day: former Indians' shortstop Felix Fermin falls to the ground after failing to turn a double play in the tenth that would have clinched a Mariners' win. (*Akron Beacon Journal*)

Although the teams had begun the afternoon with the leader of the free world in attendance, the Indians and Mariners entered extra innings on their own.

President Clinton left at the end of the ninth inning for a series of media interviews at the Sheraton City Centre Hotel before hopping on another plane. He would jet to Charlotte for that night's NCAA men's basketball championship and wrap up a sports fan's dream day: the unique doubleheader of baseball's opening day and college basketball's finale. Clinton would see a thrilling contest that evening as the Arkansas Razorbacks defeated Duke, 76-72, but he would miss the conclusion to the most exciting baseball game of the day.

Jose Mesa started off the tenth with a fastball to Ken Griffey Jr., which the pride of the Mariners fouled back into the seats. Mesa came back with another fastball that scraped the inside corner for strike one and put the twenty-seven-year-old Dominican Republic native in the driver's seat. Griffey laid off an inside slider, then ripped a grounder toward short on a fourth-pitch fastball. Omar Vizquel stopped his former teammate's shot by diving to his knees, but he couldn't quite glove it. He picked up the ball near the outfield grass, rose, and hurled it to first. Griffey beat the toss by a step for a leadoff infield single.

Opting to manage with the National League–style that had won him a World Series four years before, Lou Piniella sent Jay Buhner, a man who had hit twenty-seven home runs the year before, to the plate to bunt Griffey into scoring position. Mesa's first pitch, a slider, dipped low, and Buhner pulled the bat back. Mesa came back with a fastball that Buhner bunted perfectly down the first-base line. Murray and Mesa both ran to retrieve it and stood to watch for a moment as the ball tightroped the baseline, hinting at rolling foul. After another split second, it was still fair, and Murray snatched it up and lobbed it over the running Buhner to Carlos Baerga for the sure out at first as Griffey moved to second.

With the left-handed Eric Anthony on deck, Mike Hargrove didn't want to give him a decent shot at knocking in his third run of the day, so the Indians' fourth-year manager trotted out to the mound and signaled for southpaw Derek Lilliquist to replace Mesa.

Lilliquist was coming off two fine seasons after the Indians claimed him off waivers from San Diego in November of 1991. In '92 he was 5-3 with a 1.75 ERA and six saves. The following season he collected ten saves and a 2.25 ERA. He was expected to be one of the anchors of the Cleveland bullpen in 1994, and this was a golden opportunity to prove it.

As Lilliquist finished his warmup tosses, the shadows had stretched past the mound and swallowed the entire third-base area in darkness. "Good thing we snuck in daylight-savings time this weekend," Chris Berman noted, "or they'd be out to first base."

On his first pitch Lilliquist missed with a slider in the dirt, then enticed Anthony to pop up a deceiving curve into foul territory, where Murray caught it on the rubberized track beside first base. Even though Griffey remained at second with two down and the left-handed Tino Martinez coming up, Lilliquist was one out away from getting out of trouble.

But he appeared a bit too cautious to Martinez as he put two straight sliders in the dirt. Sandy Alomar made a nice stop on the second pitch to prevent Griffey from advancing. Another slider dipped low to put Lilliquist behind 3-and-0, and then he missed high with a curve, sending Martinez to first as a result of Seattle's first walk since the second inning.

With two on and two out, Piniella pulled back Reggie Jefferson in favor of pinch hitter Keith Mitchell (cousin of Kevin Mitchell), who had enjoyed an incredible spring training. He'd hit over .400 for most of the exhibition season and set a Mariners' record by knocking in twenty-two RBI. He'd played briefly with the Atlanta Braves during their first World Series run of the decade in 1991, but this would be his first major-league at-bat in more than two years after spending 1992 and 1993 in the minors.

With right-handed reliever Eric Plunk once again warming up in the bullpen and the go-ahead run in scoring position, traditional thinking would have led Hargrove to replace Lilliquist with Plunk. Instead Hargrove stuck with Lilliquist and took his chances.

After missing low with a slider for his sixth ball in seven pitches, Lilliquist bounced back with a slider strike down the middle to even the count. He missed with a high curve and then came back with a fastball that drifted a little too far inside.

Mitchell pounced on the mistake and ripped it to left field for a base hit as Griffey was off to the races. Just after he rounded third Albert Belle came up with the ball on a bounce and heaved it toward home, where Sandy Alomar stood at the ready. Meanwhile Ken Griffey Jr. was coming down the mountain.

Belle's throw sailed on him as he released it, and as the ball reached home plate, it was more than ten feet off the ground and still rising. Alomar once again showed his athletic prowess by leaping high into the air to snag it just as Griffey began his slide. Not giving up yet Alomar quickly swiped down between his legs with his glove in a last-ditch effort to tag the Seattle center fielder, but with no luck. Even though a good throw by Belle probably would have nailed him, Griffey had scored to give the Mariners a 3-2 lead, and the Indians weren't out of the woods yet. Martinez had moved to third, and Mitchell had taken second. Another base hit and it would take a minor miracle for the Indians to come back again.

Perhaps one batter too late Hargrove marched to the mound and called for Plunk. The run was charged to Jose Mesa, but the Martinez walk and the Mitchell single set the tone for the season for Lilliquist. He could never seem to find the rhythm that had propelled him in 1992 and 1993. He was tattooed for losses in back-to-back games by these same Mariners in Seattle in early June, and then he hit rock bottom two weeks later when he gave up a grand slam in the bottom of the ninth in Detroit to wipe out a 5-3 Cleveland lead. Lilliquist was placed on waivers after the season and was picked up by the Atlanta Braves, the team with which he had begun his career in 1989. He failed to make the Atlanta roster in 1995 and finished his career in Boston that season with a balmy 6.26 ERA in twenty-eight appearances.

In came Plunk, who was in the process of quietly replacing Lilliquist as the stalwart of the Cleveland bullpen. Picked up as a free agent in the first week of the 1992 campaign, Plunk had hurled 71⅔ innings for a pitching-depleted Tribe and turned in a 9-6 record that season with an impressive 3.64 ERA and four saves. A year later he was even better with a 2.79 ERA and fifteen saves. Now he was called in to stop the bleeding as the Indians tried to set the stage for one more opening-day comeback.

Plunk got Dan Wilson to fan at a nasty fastball up and in on the first pitch but not on the second. He blew another heater past the whiffing Wilson for strike two and then got him to tap a curve toward short, where Vizquel collected it and fired on to Murray to retire the side.

But had the damage already been done? True, Randy Johnson was out of the game, but Bobby Ayala was now in it and wanted nothing more than to start off the season at 1-0.

In the tenth, the Mariners scored one run on two hits, and there were no errors.

	1	2	3	4	5	6	7	8	9	10			R	H	E
SEATTLE	1	0	1	0	0	0	0	0	0	1			3	7	1
CLEVELAND	0	0	0	0	0	0	0	2	0				2	4	1

Now the stirring comeback the Indians had made in the eighth off Randy Johnson had a very good chance of being nothing more than a footnote of this historic contest.

But in the bowels of the new structure, one Indian was taking advantage of the new digs in a way that he couldn't have the year before. Since the top of the inning Jim Thome had been in the batting cages beneath the dugout, loosening up for about twenty minutes in preparation for a possible pinch-hit appearance. As Sandy Alomar Jr. stepped in to lead off the tenth, Thome was pounding balls into a net beneath the stands, something not possible at Cleveland Stadium. Although the visitors also had access to their own batting cages, this would turn out to be the first example of home-field advantage in the history of Jacobs Field.

Ayala would now get his first test as the newfound closer for the Mariners. In theory, he couldn't ask for a better setup as he'd be facing the seven, eight, and nine hitters of the Cleveland lineup. In reality (and retrospect) he would start the inning facing two of the best hitters to put on an Indians' uniform in a generation.

Ayala started with a curve over the outside corner for a strike on Alomar, who then laid off a splitfingered fastball inside at the knees to even the count. Ayala came back with two straight curves, both of which Alomar cut at and missed. He walked away from the plate, muttering to himself. The Mariners were now just two outs away from winning the first-ever game at Jacobs Field.

As Manny Ramirez stepped in to try to add to his heroic debut at the Jake, a rhythmic beat flowed through the new park. From high atop the left-field bleachers, John Adams pounded on his drum just as he had done for twenty years at Cleveland Stadium. "My general rule is when the Indians do something good, I try to beat the drum," Adams told the *Plain Dealer* that day. Or, as in this case, to try to encourage something good.

The Brecksville native began bringing his drum to the old ballpark in the mid-1970s and became an icon for Tribe diehards. He'd take his drum into the seats in the outfield and pound on it during key moments of the game to try to inspire the Indians to victory. Back at Cleveland Stadium he'd usually have an entire section to himself, so he never really bothered anyone who didn't want to hear him. Now at brand-new Jacobs Field he was surrounded and actually had to purchase two seats atop the bleachers: one for himself and one for his drum. No one seemed to mind now as he was pounding with all his might to help rally the Indians to victory.

Ramirez took strike one on a curve that caught the outside corner, then laid off another that dipped low. Two more curves from Ayala swung inside and outside, respectively, and put the right-hander down 3-and-1. After Ayala came set for his fifth pitch Dan Wilson called time and jogged out to the mound to speak with his pitcher. Conversing with their gloves over their mouths the Seattle battery got its signals straight, and Wilson returned to the plate for the pivotal fifth toss. It was a curve that didn't snap and hung high and inside for ball four, and Manny Ramirez was on base, representing the tying run.

Here Mike Hargrove made two key moves. He replaced Ramirez with the speedier Wayne Kirby, who had held the right-field job the year before and was expected to be the starting right fielder in the offseason before Ramirez caught fire in March. Hargrove then pulled back Mark Lewis in favor of left-handed— and warmed-up—Jim Thome, the young third baseman the club had such high expectations for. After three straight seasons of being called up to the major-league level before he was ready, Thome was poised for a breakthrough season, and the Tribe brass was hoping he could kick it off in a big way.

Not about to be checkmated, Lou Piniella called for lefty Kevin King to replace Ayala, who had certainly done everything the Mariners could have asked on this day. It would prove to be a sign of things to come for Ayala, who would save eighteen games in forty-six appearances in 1994 with a 2.86 ERA. While Piniella was clearly playing the percentages by putting in a southpaw to face an inexperienced left-handed batter, this move opened the door of opportunity for the Indians even wider. The three batters Ayala had faced hadn't even touched the ball, and although he let Ramirez slip away on five pitches he fanned power threats Sorrento and Alomar. If Ayala truly was going to be Seattle's closer, this would have been a perfect opportunity to field-test him. Instead Piniella called on King, who had pitched briefly and poorly for Seattle the year before, to face the 1993 International League Player of the Year.

King went ahead 0-and-1 with a fastball over the inside corner, then zeroed in on first, knowing Kirby could be a dangerous baserunner. He threw over to Tino Martinez twice, keeping Kirby close. Kirby had stolen seventeen bases with the Indians in 1993 but had swiped more than twenty-five in a season eight times in his eleven-year minor-league career. The streak included fifty-one steals with Colorado Springs in 1992 and fifty-six with Bakersfield in 1987. King knew a steal here could prove costly, so he kept his eye on the Indians' pinch runner as he prepared to make his third pitch to Thome.

Piniella looked like a genius when Thome took a big cut and miss at a looping curve that flopped out of the strike zone to put the Indian down 1-and-2. With a pitch left to play with, King tried to get Thome to chase another curve. The thinking was sound, but the execution was not.

King's curve hung inside, where Thome turned on it hard. He cranked the ball fair down the right-field line, where it bounced twice on the outfield grass, then smacked up against the right-field wall as the crowd exploded. Kirby was tearing his way around second as Jay Buhner neared the ball in the corner, and Thome veered toward second. Buhner made an outstanding read, grabbed the ball on one bounce off the wall, and quickly fired it to Martinez near first. Buhner's quickness forced Kirby to put on the brakes at third. Had the ball taken one more bounce or had Buhner been half as fooled as Eric Anthony was on Ramirez's double to left in the eighth, the game would have been tied. Instead Kirby was at third, and Thome was at second with one out and Kenny Lofton stepping up to bat.

The luxury of the underground batting cages had paid off on day one. "I went right from there to the dugout," Thome told the *Beacon Journal*. "Maybe a minute went by before I got up to hit, and I was loose and ready."

Knowing Thome represented the winning run Piniella had King intentionally walk Lofton to load the bases and create a potential double play for Seattle. Piniella would take his chances with the man who had been his starting shortstop the year before, Omar Vizquel.

As the switch-hitting Vizquel settled into the box the throng at Jacobs Field rose to its feet, understanding that no matter what Vizquel did in this at-bat it would have a huge impact on the outcome of the game. It would be the first true pressure plate appearance in Jacobs Field history. And it would live up to its expectation.

King missed low and inside with a curve. The crowd grew even giddier, and the pressure and intensity grew by the second. They needed wait only for the next pitch, a curveball that King hung down the center.

Vizquel hit a screamer right back up the middle that King fanned at with his left hand as he came back up on his follow-through. The crowd roared even louder in the next half-second, foreseeing the ball streaking through the infield and into center field, possibly clinching an Indians' victory.

But Rich Amaral came out of nowhere, dove to his right, and snared it off the ground behind second, landing flat on his stomach. In that instant Amaral exemplified one of the beauties of baseball crunch time: his athletic play prevented the Mariners from losing the game then and there, and a split-second later he gave the Mariners a chance to win it—right then and there.

As Kirby crossed home plate Amaral rolled on his back and tossed the ball to Felix Fermin covering second. Fermin caught Amaral's toss as he tagged second with his foot and cocked his arm to throw to first as Kenny Lofton bore down on him like a cheetah in a bad mood. As Fermin reached into his glove to begin his throw to first to potentially end the game, Lofton slid into his shins. Fermin jumped up to try to avoid him, but there was contact. The ball popped out of his hand and fell to the ground, with Fermin crashing down after it. Lofton's hustle had rescued Vizquel from a certain double play.

Almost before the ball hit the dirt, Lou Piniella was racing up the dugout steps and out onto the field. "That's fucking interference!" he screamed, running out to second base at about the same rate of speed that Kenny Lofton had ten seconds earlier.

Second-base umpire Al Clark said no, it wasn't interference, and much to Piniella's chagrin replays showed that not only was Lofton's slide within the designated leeway of the bag, but that Fermin had been bobbling the ball out of his glove before Lofton made contact. When the dust settled and Piniella returned to the dugout, Kirby's run counted, and the Indians had once again come back to tie the game. Even better, they would now have a chance to win it with Thome at third, Vizquel at first, and Carlos Baerga coming up.

Just in case Indians' fans didn't think that the Vizquel-Fermin trade wasn't going to have a major impact on both franchises, the baseball gods had sent a strikingly obvious memo to the contrary on that previous play. On what would turn out to be the most critical at-bat of the afternoon (even more so than Ramirez's eighth-inning double), the outcome of the game had hung on both of these players' shoulders within five seconds. First, Vizquel came through with a smash to extend the game, although Rich Amaral had nearly made it a moot point. Then, a moment later, Fermin bungled the double play, and, thus, in the key moment of opening day, the Indians got the better half of the trade. This play would also seem to serve as a turning point in both players' careers, and, consequently, the fork in the road in the franchises' fortunes over the next few seasons.

To Kevin King's credit he zeroed back in on the task at hand when he could have mentally headed for the showers. Facing Baerga, the toughest young switch hitter in the American League, he missed low with a curve on the first pitch, setting up another curve that doglegged outside but got Baerga to chase. Baerga popped the ball into medium center, where Griffey gloved it. The game would continue as afternoon began its soft transition to evening.

In the tenth, the Indians scored one run on one hit, and there were no errors.

THE ELEVENTH

	1	2	3	4	5	6	7	8	9	10	11		R	H	E
SEATTLE	1	0	1	0	0	0	0	0	0	1			3	7	1
CLEVELAND	0	0	0	0	0	0	0	2	0	1			3	5	1

Seattle center fielder Ken Griffey Jr. slides beneath the tag of Sandy Alomar to score the go-ahead run in the top of the tenth inning. (*Akron Beacon Journal*)

Eric Plunk stayed on the mound following his tenth-inning heroics, as did Jim Thome at third and Wayne Kirby in right. With the game now entering another phase and yet another level of pressure, it is ironic that Plunk had one of the easiest innings of the afternoon for any pitcher on either side.

He followed a low curve with a fastball at the letters to even the count on Felix Fermin. The Seattle shortstop sliced another fastball into the first-base seats and then popped one up on the left side of the infield, where it was caught behind the mound, naturally, by Omar Vizquel. Fermin was now 0-for-5 on the day.

With shadows covering first and second base, Plunk and Eddie Murray pulled off a deceptively difficult play. After Rich Amaral laid off a high fastball he dropped a bunt into the no-man's-land between the mound and home plate, where either Sandy Alomar or Plunk would have to travel as far as he possibly could to pick it up. Plunk got there first and scooped it up methodically. He fired through the patches of shadow toward first, where Murray kept his eye on the ball and snagged it an instant before the speedy Amaral reached the bag. Though a ball thrown by a teammate is much easier to follow than a line drive hit by an opponent, Murray faced a problem similar to Mark Lewis's in Amaral's last at-bat— the double down the third-base line in the ninth. Unlike the younger Lewis, no matter how new the ballpark in which he was playing not much in baseball could surprise Eddie Murray.

With two out Mike Blowers stepped to the plate. By now it seemed like a season had passed since Blowers had replaced Edgar Martinez at third after he took a fastball to the wrist in the first inning. Blowers swung at and missed Plunk's first curve, then laid off a breaker that dipped low. He fouled a fastball into the first-base seats, then Plunk missed with a curve low and away to even the count at 2-and-2. After Blowers ripped another fastball into the seats, Plunk got him to go after a sinister curveball that ducked out of the strike zone precisely at the perfect moment, leaving Blowers with an empty swing.

Retiring all four batters he'd faced, Plunk had done the job, as he would continue to do out of the Cleveland bullpen. He would have the best year of his career in 1994, going 7-2 with a 2.54 ERA and three saves in forty-one appearances. He would turn in two more seasons with an ERA under three in 1995 and 1996 before things would start to sour. In 1997 he went 4-5 with a 4.66 ERA in a faltering bullpen, and after another shaky start in 1998 he was traded to Milwaukee in July for a blast from the Indians' past: Doug Jones, Cleveland's all-time save leader.

But in the first-ever game at Jacobs Field, Plunk was about to have his name immortalized in the history of Major League Baseball's newest jewel.

	1	2	3	4	5	6	7	8	9	10	11			R	H	E
SEATTLE	1	0	1	0	0	0	0	0	0	1	0			3	7	1
CLEVELAND	0	0	0	0	0	0	0	2	0	1				3	5	1

For the second time in three innings Albert Belle stepped to the plate with the opportunity to send everybody home with one swing.

Leading off the bottom of the eleventh, Belle took three straight balls outside from Kevin King: two fastballs sandwiched around a curve. With the green light on 3-and-0, Belle made a rare mistake. He swung at an inside fastball that cracked off the handle of his bat wide of first, where Tino Martinez gloved it and jogged to the bag for the first out. Belle had let King off the hook. But Eddie Murray would make up for it.

Eddie Murray, a switch-hitter, batting from the right side, Herb Score told his listeners. *Bottom of the eleventh inning, we are tied. And the pitch . . .*

It was a breaking ball that didn't break as much as King had in mind. Murray crushed it to deep left-center field as the crowd sprang to its feet.

Drive deep to left field!

Certain that the ball was out of the park Murray hesitated at home plate for a moment before slowly beginning to trot to first. While Ken Griffey Jr. scampered with his back to home plate, the crowd seemed as convinced as Murray as it swelled to a crescendo.

Back goes Griffey! He's at the wall!

But in a twist of realistic fortune everyone was reminded that, although this was the same town where Frank Robinson had performed one of the most dramatic moments in baseball history nineteen years earlier, it still wasn't Hollywood. True, the new ballpark and the new Indians seemed like a match made in heaven, but there was still going to be a honeymoon period.

Griffey leaps . . . it's off the wall!

Murray's blast pounded twelve feet up into the nineteen-foot wall in left center and out of the reach of a leaping Griffey. As Murray reached first base he realized that Jacobs' Ladder had just pulled rank on him, and he started steaming toward second.

Into second base goes Eddie Murray.

The ball bounded away from Griffey back toward straightaway center. But, ever the athlete, he was quickly on top of it and fired it back in before Murray could think about taking third.

He makes the turn, he'll stay right there. The Indians with a runner at second.

A better jump out of the batter's box might have put Murray ninety feet from victory, but no Tribe fan would dare criticize the thirty-eight-year-old veteran for only reaching second on a shot off the wall.

While Murray's bat was showing Cleveland backers that he was no has-been free-agent acquisition—à la Keith Hernandez in 1990—Dennis Martinez was doing the same. Still in the dugout, wearing a jacket and toting a towel and hot-water bag, Martinez was the first player standing on the Indians' bench when Murray made contact. The combination of the hit and the reaction by two of the most respected players in the game seemed to be one more piece of symbolism in a day already saturated with it.

The crowd was once again going bonkers. After nearly ending this whole thing in the ninth, when his potential run-scoring hit landed a hair foul, Murray had now put the Indians a safety away from triumph number one at Jacobs Field.

Eddie Murray missed ending this game by a couple of feet.

Just as was the case in the Indians' first game at Cleveland Stadium, the home team had been robbed of an outcome-altering home run in the late innings. On that sunny day in 1932 it was Eddie *Morgan* who blasted a shot in the ninth inning that would have cleared the lofty right-field wall at League Park but instead settled into Bing Miller's glove to seal a 1-0 win for the Philadelphia Athletics. Although Murray's hit still put the Indians in a position to win the ballgame, the torch of baseball irony had officially been passed in Cleveland, Ohio.

With victory 180 feet away, Paul Sorrento stepped to the plate, hoping to atone for his strikeout in the ninth with Belle at third. After taking a low breaking ball, it appeared he had done more than that. Sorrento ripped another King breaker toward center, and for a moment it seemed like a replay of Murray's at-bat, with Griffey sprinting backwards once again. But a split-second later, Griffey slowed down under the ball on the warning track and caught it, then fired back to the infield. Murray, who had remained at second, now tagged and headed for third, which was completely engulfed in shadows. He made it there easily, even though he stumbled six feet away from the base and nearly fell into it as Griffey's throw reached Blowers a few feet off the bag.

The good news was that Murray was now just ninety feet from home. The bad news was that there were two outs, and with Sandy Alomar stepping to the plate and Wayne Kirby on deck Piniella did what was natural: he had King intentionally walk Alomar.

At 4:48 P.M. Wayne Kirby stepped into the batter's box. The man who had spent more than a decade in the minors before finally breaking in with the Indians a year earlier would now decide whether his team won its first-ever game at Jacobs Field here and now, or if it would toil on into the gently falling dusk.

Just before Kirby stepped into the on-deck circle, Jim Thome—scheduled to follow Kirby should he extend the inning—advised him to look for outside fastballs from King.

On the first pitch Kirby laid off an inside curve as Alomar raced into second with no effort to throw him out. Kirby went ahead 2-and-0 when a curve dipped low and a trifle outside. Things looked even better for the Indians when King's third-pitch fastball sank low and outside to put Kirby ahead 3-and-0. Not about to get burned twice in one inning Hargrove gave Kirby the red light for King's fourth pitch, a curve that appeared to drop below the knees. But Barnett, as if making up for the borderline ball-two call, judged it a strike, and the crowd "ooh"-ed as Dan Wilson tossed the ball back to King.

Kirby kept moving in the batter's box, never taking his eyes off King. He twirled his bat in a circular motion, keeping loose and focused. King zeroed in on Wilson, twitching the ball in his left hand. As King came set, Kirby finished his bat's final rotation and stood completely still.

At 4:50 P.M. on April 4, 1994, Kevin King wound and delivered the 336th pitch of the first game at Jacobs Field.

It was, as Thome had suggested, an outside fastball.

Three balls and a strike, Score announced, *here's the pitch . . .*

Kirby swung and drove it off the inside portion of his bat over third, cutting toward the left-field line. Blowers leapt for it, but the ball was a good six feet over his head and about to begin sinking. He never raised his arms on the jump; then, as he realized the fate of the baseball, he returned to the ground as his shoulders deflated.

Line drive! Left field!

As the ball soared over Blowers's head, Eddie Murray raised his arms and started trotting home. A moment later third-base coach Jeff Newman raised his arms. Eric Anthony pursued the ball, but it dropped fifteen feet to the right of the left-field line. Under ordinary circumstances it would have been a double.

Base hit! The game is over! The Indians win it! Wayne Kirby coming through with an eleventh-inning base hit!

Kirby ran down to first to complete the transaction, then headed back toward home plate.

As Murray neared home Dan Wilson began to stand up, but only halfway, and stared at home plate, just to make sure that Murray touched it. He did, and for a moment it appeared as if Wilson were bowing to the thirty-eight-year-old veteran as he scored the winning run.

The Tribe a victory today, 4-3, in the first game ever at Jacobs Field!

In the eleventh, the Indians scored one run on two hits, and there were no errors.

POSTGAME

	1	2	3	4	5	6	7	8	9	10	11		R	H	E
SEATTLE	1	0	1	0	0	0	0	0	0	1	0		3	7	1
CLEVELAND	0	0	0	0	0	0	0	2	0	1	1		4	7	1

Pitcher Charles Nagy—who would symbolize the Indians' steady-as-she-goes success in the late 1990s—signs autographs before the first game at Jacobs Field. (*Akron Beacon Journal*)

As Wayne Kirby jogged back toward home Jeff Newman ran across the infield to become the second to congratulate him; first-base coach Dave Nelson had been the first. Eddie Murray crossed home plate and high-fived Jim Thome, who had been on deck. When Kirby reached home plate he was swarmed by his teammates. Sandy Alomar foreshadowed celebrations to come when he quickly (and lightly) pounded Kirby on the batting helmet. It would be the first of many headaches for Indians who came through in the clutch at Jacobs Field.

"The Indians got a little bit of everything today," ESPN's Buck Martinez said, and the variety of celebrations following Kirby's hit symbolized that statement.

Kenny Lofton was the first player up off the Indians' bench when Kirby's hit rocketed into left field. Paul Sorrento raised one arm in triumph. Albert Belle raised both as he climbed onto the dugout steps. Carlos Baerga hopped up the steps and out onto the rubberized track, clapping. He gave his new double-play partner, Omar Vizquel, a high-five, and they embraced.

The crowd roared during the celebration, and in the next few minutes, people slowly started making their way out of Jacobs Field, just in time to sit in rush-hour traffic downtown. Meanwhile the players headed to their respective locker rooms. They knew they'd been part of something special, but even the Indians didn't know quite how special.

"It felt good to take advantage of the park," Belle told the *Beacon Journal,* "to take the first step in making it a tough place for a team to come in here and win. I think we showed that today."

"This is my fifth year here and it's the first time we won the first game," Alomar added. "Hopefully that means something."

The victory wasn't the only thing that seemed to promise brighter days ahead. The Indians could also be proud of several other facets of the contest.

For starters, two players at one position came up with the biggest hits of the game: right fielders Manny Ramirez and Wayne Kirby. Longtime fans could only wonder when the Indians had last been deep enough to have two talented players at one position and have both be heroes in the same game. A conservative guess was 1954.

"I'm pretty happy things came out the way they did," Kirby said. "I had a good spring, and when Mike [Hargrove] gave me the word [that Ramirez would start], I took it kind of hard. The first day worked out fine for me. I just hope it continues."

Kirby told the *Plain Dealer,* "I'm going to play my heart out and do everything I can to get [playing time]. But if Manny continues to do well, I'm stuck with being a bench player. And I can accept that right now."

It truly had been a good day for Kirby, but it was also the beginning of the end of his career in Cleveland. He proved to be a valuable factor off the bench for the Tribe in 1994 and 1995, but with the team's depth swelling he was eventually placed on waivers in June 1996 and claimed by the Los Angeles Dodgers. He would see limited action off the bench in forthcoming seasons with the Dodgers, Mets, and Orioles. Kirby's younger brother, Terry, who broke into the National Football League as a running back, similarly started for the Cleveland Browns in their first game at their new stadium in September 1999.

The situation couldn't have worked out better for Hargrove. His decision to start Ramirez was immediately justified but didn't keep Kirby from seeing that he still had a role to play on this team, at least for the immediate future.

"Even when things don't break right for Wayne, he keeps a good attitude, and it's guys with talent and character who come through," Hargrove said in the *Plain Dealer.* "I don't want to sound like this is the end of the world. This is the first of 162. But I'm glad we won because it sure beats the alternative."

For a while that afternoon the alternative had been far worse than just losing. "A no-hitter on opening day would have been the biggest headline in baseball this year," Alomar said, and he wasn't exaggerating. Just ask Bob Feller.

"I worked with what I had and gave what I had and made it interesting," said a disappointed Randy Johnson in the *Plain Dealer.* "That's the way it goes. I'm pretty pleased."

He told the *Beacon Journal,* "It was kind of a slow day for both teams. We didn't play our best, and I'm sure the Indians don't feel they played their best."

The Indians admitted that they'd been truly scared of being victims of history once Johnson reached the middle innings. They realized that they might have missed their best opportunities to get to Johnson early in the contest. "He started off just okay, mostly mixing up his pitches," Belle added. "But in the fourth, fifth, and sixth innings, he really started to cut loose."

Although it was obvious that Johnson was waning by the time the Indians got to him in the eighth, it was the first time all day that he had looked truly vulnerable, and the Indians took advantage at precisely the right moment. "It didn't seem to me that Johnson was tired," Hargrove said. "But he sure was making us tired."

But how much of the Indians' offensive ineptitude through seven innings was due to Johnson's skill and how much was due to his commanding presence alone? "I hear that all the time and I'm tired of it," Johnson barked. "I don't know if guys are intimidated when they face me or not. I really can't answer a question about me."

New teammate Felix Fermin probably summed up the situation best. "I'm telling you," he said, "facing Randy Johnson is no fun."

Although the Indians' batters may not have been having much fun, their fans certainly were. Most were very impressed with the new ballpark, but conversely, Ken Griffey Jr. didn't have much glowing praise to offer. Just as Babe Ruth didn't have much nice to say about Cleveland Stadium in 1932, Griffey said in the *Beacon Journal* that Jacobs Field was "just another place to play ball." Maybe there's something in the premier power hitters of each generation that just can't accept the beauty of a new yard. Or maybe Griffey was frustrated that his club had held victory in its hands multiple times and simply couldn't hold onto it.

"There were three times when I thought we had the game lost," Indians' owner Richard Jacobs said. "Our guys came through in exemplary fashion, which really made me happy for the folks in the community."

Now that Jacobs Field was reality and its first game was history, all involved had to shift gears back into the everyday grind of baseball. Although it was special, dramatic, and exciting, in the final analysis, it was one game. Following this one in the coming months were supposed to be 161 more, including 80 more in this unfamiliar new landmark.

"It's like buying a house," bleacher drum-beater John Adams said in the *Beacon Journal*. "When you first move in, it's not really your house. You have to move things in and make it your place. So it's here, but it's not mine yet. But we'll make this home."

As the players left Jacobs Field and the magical atmosphere that had prevailed for nearly six hours drifted back into the heavens, a wonderful mixture of reality and nostalgia seemed to trickle into the hearts of Indians' fans everywhere. They came to the park thinking about history—the people, the games, and the stories that had come before. By game's end they were looking toward a future that was much brighter than they'd seen in more than forty years. But they also realized not every day would be as poetic as this one.

The Indians would not—could not—win every game, no matter how nice a ballpark they were playing in. Soon the drudgery of the regular season would begin, and one day amazement at the sight of Jacobs Field would fade and be replaced by apathy from many who passed through its gates. It was inevitable.

But the true fans would always have the memories of this day to carry with them. No matter what the Indians did in the future, no one could ever take away their epic, almost romantic, first-ever opening day at Jacobs Field and their dramatic win. It was a game that had a little of everything, and regardless of where the team went in the standings in the future, the score "Indians 4, Mariners 3," would always burn brightly in thousands of memories, including those of fans not present to witness the event firsthand.

At the dawn of an era of baseball that is dominated by mass-media revenue, luxury loges, and huge, free-agency spending, Jacobs Field would turn out to be more than a tourist attraction and result in more than just a big first year at the gate. It would soon become an angel of mercy, resting at the corner of Ontario and Carnegie and, much like Jesus did for Lazarus, it would bring a franchise and a generation of baseball fans in Northeast Ohio back from the dead.

CLIMBING JACOBS'S LADDER

"Think about it for a moment," Terry Pluto wrote in the *Akron Beacon Journal* following the Indians' victory over Seattle. "How many times did the Indians go out and spoil a perfectly good day like this one? How many times did they tease you, then tear your heart out?"

There is no answer, because no one could possibly count that high and not start conversing with the furniture.

Pluto brought up an excellent point. The script, even in the new ballpark with new uniforms and new players, was written. The die had been cast, even on a sunny April day in Cleveland, one without rain or snow or boneheaded trades or strippers or calendars-turned-paper airplanes.

The Indians were supposed to lose this game.

They were given every opportunity to shatter what would have otherwise been a magnificent occasion. They had faced Randy Johnson, baseball's best pitcher, with his good stuff going. Eric Anthony, a man who would drive in just thirty runs over the course of the season to come had somehow managed to produce two within the first three innings for the visitors. A couple of calls didn't go the Indians' way. A couple of line drives hung up in the thin spring air and were caught. Just one of these setbacks would have been enough to defeat the old Indians, the team that took the field in Cleveland from 1960 through 1993.

But two crucial at-bats had changed the script, and Sandy Alomar's single in the eighth to break up the no-hitter wasn't one of them.

The first critical moment immediately followed Alomar's hit: Manny Ramirez's double off the left-field wall that scored two runs and tied the game. While ending the no-hitter was important, the old Indians probably would have managed it somewhere along the line, then folded up the tents, satisfied at avoiding too embarrassing a place in history. Ramirez changed three decades of ineptitude with one swing of the bat.

Although they may not have admitted it afterward, most fans probably felt not only relieved but also satisfied when Alomar got the hit to break up the no-hitter. At least the Indians wouldn't be the lead story on ESPN's *SportsCenter* for something that humiliating. Many fans had already accepted defeat by the time Alomar made that hit and just wanted the team to get out relatively unharmed from a historic standpoint. Then Ramirez, a twenty-one-year-old rookie, facing Johnson for just the third time in his career, tore the script in half.

It didn't matter that he blew a chance for the Indians to win the game by getting picked off a few moments later. The prince of the Indians' farm system showed everyone in Cleveland that a new era was under way. This script, this team, this park were all brand new. And the Indians wanted the city to come along for the ride.

The second key at-bat was Omar Vizquel's RBI fielder's choice in the tenth that tied the game. As Pluto said, the Indians had teased their fans once again. They'd rallied back from a deficit against the best pitcher in baseball, but after a couple of bad breaks in the top of the tenth, it all appeared for naught. An Indians' loss in ten after an admirable comeback would not have been as damaging as a no-hitter, but it would have been a familiar outcome to many fans. "Yeah, they're better, but . . . "

Vizquel's shot up the middle would have been a double play had Felix Fermin not bobbled the ball after getting the first out at second, but it was anything but a routine ground ball. Rich Amaral had made the defensive play of the day to prevent the game from ending right there. What if Vizquel had chopped a lazy grounder to second in that situation and the Mariners *had* turned the double play to end the game? It would have seemed only appropriate to longtime Tribe fans. The new guy for whom the Indians gave up a perfectly adequate shortstop chokes in the clutch, while the guy they gave up turns the double play to beat them in their first game in the new ballpark. Instead Vizquel came through with a line drive that scored Wayne Kirby from third to tie the game and send it to the eleventh. Plus, if Amaral had been leaning in the other direction for a split-second longer or had been two inches farther to his left, Vizquel would have been the game's hero, not Wayne Kirby.

The two players who came through in these two history-changing at-bats would go on to play tremendous roles in the production that was to take center stage at Jacobs Field over the remainder of the decade.

After a snowout the following Wednesday the Indians' Jack Morris defeated Chris Bosio on Thursday night, 6-2, in game two at Jacobs Field, thanks in part to Eddie Murray's solo home run in the seventh, the Indians' first in their new home. The Tribe then went West, splitting a pair in Kansas City before sweeping the Angels in Anaheim to move to 6-1 on the season. It certainly appeared that the new park was having an immediate impact. But the club returned home and was swept by the Royals, beginning a monthlong stretch of inconsistency that recalled the old Indians. After a jarring four-game sweep at the hands of the

Yankees in New York the second week of May, the Indians returned to Jacobs Field in fourth place at 14-17, apparently heading, as usual, nowhere.

Then a 2-0 complete-game victory by Cleveland's Mark Clark to open a series with the Tigers at the Jake sparked a dramatic turnaround. An offensive eruption by the Indians led to 9-3 and 11-6 wins the next two days, and the Tribe was off and running. The Indians slowly moved up in the standings and eventually caught the White Sox in a tie for first on June 12. Chicago slumped, while the Indians' lead grew to 4½ games on the strength of a ten-game winning streak. Although that string soon snapped, another even more impressive kept going. Since the Indians' win over Detroit to open the series that turned the season around on May 13, they rattled off eighteen consecutive home victories through June 25, the longest home winning streak in baseball in six years. Included in that stretch was a wild 7-6 win over Boston on June 16, when the Indians rallied from two down in the ninth to beat the Red Sox and go on to sweep the four-game series.

The White Sox came back to tie the Indians on July 8 to set up two of the most exciting regular-season series for these clubs since they played a quartet at Cleveland Stadium in September 1959 to decide that year's pennant. The teams split a crazy four-game set in Chicago July 14–17, during which the umpires confiscated Albert Belle's bat to investigate it for cork. During that game, it was revealed years later, Indians' relief pitcher Jason Grimsley crawled through a vent from the Indians' locker room to the umpires' dressing room at Comiskey Park and replaced Belle's bat (that *was* corked) with another. Grimsley's *Mission: Impossible* routine didn't work. The original bat was eventually returned to the umps, and Belle was found out and suspended for seven games.

With tension as thick as a swarm of mosquitoes off the lake, the Indians and White Sox again faced off for four July 21–24, a weekend series in Cleveland. With Jacobs Field packed to capacity the teams split another pair, but the highlight was an 11-2 dumping the Indians tagged on Chicago in the Saturday contest. The White Sox left Cleveland leading the Indians by two games, but the Tribe would catch them again July 28 and take over sole possession of first place a day later, only to fall out of the top spot the next day with a loss to the Yankees. It would be the Indians' last claim to first place that year.

With the Indians and White Sox nearing the home stretch of what was shaping up to be the most exciting pennant race for either team since Richard Nixon was vice president, Major League Baseball's owners and the Players Association were having trouble coming to terms on a new contract. The negotiations had been going nowhere since the previous offseason, and if the sides didn't reach a settlement by midnight on August 12 the players would strike. Sure enough, following a

5-3 Indians' win in Toronto on August 10 (moving them to 66-47, one game be-hind Chicago) the players walked out and the season was put on hold.

Most fans figured that the sides would come to an agreement before October and at least preserve the new playoffs and World Series. Cleveland fans would have been satisfied with that since the Indians had fended off a late run by Kansas City to hold on to the wild-card spot. They would have qualified for the playoffs had they started up on a dime.

But they didn't. The 1994 season came to an end with the Indians holding a remarkable 35-16 record at home. A total of 1,995,174 fans came to see them at Jacobs Field, which sold out thirty-six times. But the curtain also came down on a campaign with no postseason, and for the three-zillionth time in thirty-four years Cleveland was left with the short end of the stick.

By March 1995 it didn't appear that having a new ballpark in Cleveland would matter at all. The players and owners still hadn't reached a deal, and far-inferior replacement players were being groomed in Florida and Arizona to take over for the real ones. The parties finally reached an eleventh-hour agreement, and the season began with real players three weeks late. In front of not-surprisingly small crowds, the Tribe got off to a great start at 18-9 before Chicago, the only true threat to the Indians in the Central, came to Cleveland for a four-game series. After trailing the White Sox 6-0 in the opener on a gloomy Memorial Day after-noon, a home run by the venerable Dave Winfield, whom general manager John Hart had acquired in the oblivion of the strike, sparked the Indians to a 7-6 win. They went on to sweep the series and take a six-game lead in the division. By the All-Star break the lead was twelve games, and the Indians were coasting toward the postseason.

Led by the red-hot Albert Belle, who would become the first man ever to hit fifty home runs and fifty doubles in the same season, the Indians looked even better in the second half as they clearly became the best team in baseball. With a solid starting pitching staff of Dennis Martinez, Orel Hershiser, Charles Nagy, Mark Clark, and trade-deadline acquisition Ken Hill, plus a lineup that made opposing pitchers wake up at night screaming, the Indians were almost untouch-able. After failing to settle on a closer, in 1994 Jose Mesa stepped into the role and embraced it, saving a team-record forty-six games, including a major-league record thirty-eight in a row without a blown save. Mesa's success set up the rest of the bullpen, which turned out to be the best in franchise history. In a strike-shortened 144-game schedule, the Indians won 100 games and clinched their first playoff appearance in forty-one years with a 3-2 home win over Baltimore on September 8 at Jacobs Field.

The 1995 postseason would be the first under the new, tri-division format, and the Indians were matched with the Boston Red Sox in the first series, which was best of five. In one of the most memorable games in franchise history, the Indians defeated Boston, 5-4, in thirteen innings in Game One on a two-out Tony Pena home run at 2:08 in the morning. A two-run double in the fifth by Omar Vizquel the next night led to a 4-0 victory and a two-games-to-none lead in the series. The Indians crushed the Red Sox at Fenway in Game Three to advance to the American League Championship Series for the first time ever. As the Indians ventured into uncharted waters, they would face the same team that had helped them inaugurate their new home and begin their journey—the Seattle Mariners.

After splitting the opening games in the Kingdome, the teams returned to Cleveland for Game Three, a contest eerily similar to opening day, 1994. Randy Johnson took the mound for Seattle—against Charles Nagy this time—and took an early 2-0 advantage. Just as they'd done eighteen months before, the Indians tied it at two in the eighth, and the game wasn't decided until the eleventh inning. But this time it was the Mariners who came out on top, as Jay Buhner hit a three-run home run off Eric Plunk to move Seattle to within two wins of the World Series. The Indians rallied back with a 7-0 win the next night to tie the series, then the teams squared off in one of the most thrilling games ever played at Jacobs Field.

After the Indians took an early lead on a Sunday night in Game Five, Seattle snuck into a 2-1 lead in the fifth. Jim Thome clobbered a two-run home run off Chris Bosio in the sixth to give the Tribe a 3-2 lead, and then it got some outstanding pitching and stellar defense. With runners at second and third and one out in the seventh, reliever Paul Assenmacher struck out Ken Griffey Jr. and Jay Buhner back-to-back to get out of trouble. In the eighth, with Mariners on second and third and one out, Luis Sojo hit a screamer up the middle that seemed destined to score both runs and give Seattle the lead. But Vizquel was in the right spot at the right time to snare the line drive and then tag out Alex Diaz to end the inning. The contest ended when Edgar Martinez blasted a drive off Mesa to the deepest part of center field, where Kenny Lofton gloved it two feet from the wall. The Indians were now just one win away from the Series, but they had to return to Seattle and face Johnson in Game Six.

It would be a pitching rematch from the first game at Jacobs Field, as an aching Dennis Martinez took the mound at the Kingdome. It had been a long season for the forty-year old veteran, and now he needed to come up with a gem to give the Tribe a chance to beat Johnson. If he couldn't, Game Seven would fall in the lap of Nagy, who had a horrific record in the Kingdome. Martinez was up to the challenge. He held the Mariners scoreless for seven innings, and his offense gave him a 1-0 lead in the fourth. In the eighth Pena led off with a double for the Indians and was replaced by Ruben Amaro. Lofton laid down a bunt single to move Amaro to third in front of an agitated Johnson, then stole second. Johnson's next pitch sailed over the head of Dan Wilson and to the backstop, scoring Amaro—and Lofton. The Cleveland center fielder never stopped when he reached third, as Wilson took his time getting the loose ball. Lofton slid into home under a lackadaisical tag attempt from a weary Johnson. It gave the Indians a 3-0 lead, and after Carlos Baerga followed with a solo home run, the Indians were on their way to the World Series on the strength of Martinez's first-ever postseason victory and the biggest win of his twenty-year career.

Lofton was at it again in Game One of the World Series in Atlanta as he scored in the first inning on an error, two stolen bases, and a ground out. Unfortunately that was all the offense the Indians could muster off Braves' starter Greg Maddux until the ninth inning, when Lofton again scored without a hit. The Braves won, 3-2. The Tribe took an early 2-0 lead in Game Two on an Eddie Murray homer, but Atlanta came back to tie it in the third and grabbed a 4-2 advantage in the sixth. The Indians cut the lead to one in the seventh, and Manny Ramirez reached first with one out in the eighth, representing the tying run. But just as in the eighth inning of the first game at Jacobs Field the young Ramirez was picked off (this time by Atlanta catcher Javy Lopez), and Cleveland fell behind two games to none.

After the Indians appeared to have victory in hand with a 4-1 lead going into the sixth inning of Game Three at Jacobs Field, the Braves rallied back to take a 6-5 lead in the eighth. The 1995 Indians were suddenly looking very much like their 1954 predecessors, who were swept away by the New York Giants in the Fall Classic. But an eighth-inning double by Sandy Alomar tied the game, and an Eddie Murray single in the eleventh scored Alvaro Espinoza and gave the Tribe its first victory in a World Series game in forty-seven years. The Indians went down quietly, 5-2, in Game Four, and now their backs were to the wall with Maddux set to take the mound for Game Five. A first-inning two-run homer by Albert Belle followed by a Maddux brush-back of Murray seemed to recharge the Indians' batteries, and an eighth-inning Jim Thome bomb turned out to be the difference in Cleveland's 5-4 win, which sent the series back to Atlanta.

A sixth-inning home run by David Justice off Indians' reliever Jim Poole gave the Braves all the offense they'd need behind the untouchable Tom Glavine in Game Six. Glavine held Cleveland to just one hit, a single by Pena in the sixth. When Carlos Baerga was retired on a fly out to left to end the game, the Indians' fabulous 1995 run was over, but everyone seemed to feel this was just the beginning. The 1995 Tribe was just the first of what many thought would be a dynasty of champions at Jacobs Field.

The dynasty was delayed somewhat the following year. Despite the impressive offseason acquisitions of starting pitcher Jack McDowell and first baseman Julio Franco, the 1996 Indians just couldn't live up to the standard set by the 1995 team. Still they won ninety-nine games, ran away with the Central Division, and once again appeared to be the team to beat in the AL playoffs. Due to the obscenity of the early organization—or rather lack thereof—of the new playoff structure, the Indians, who held the best record in baseball, had to go on the road for the first two games of the division series with the Baltimore Orioles. The Indians were to host the potential final three games of the series, but this was counter to the typical sports postseason structure of home-field advantage in a five-game series: first two at home, the next two away, and the deciding game at home. This change made all the difference for the Orioles.

It appeared that Baltimore would be without star second baseman Roberto Alomar, who had spit in the face of home-plate umpire John Hirschbeck during an argument in the final series of the regular season. But as was the usual procedure when a player is suspended by the league, Alomar appealed, and his suspension would wait for a hearing. He was permitted to play against the Indians in the playoffs.

Game One started seventeen minutes late because of an umpire walkout over the league's handling of the incident. Brady Anderson eventually led off the Baltimore first inning with a homer, a sign of things to come. Cleveland starter Nagy and a shaky bullpen just didn't have it, and the Orioles took the lead in the series with a 10-4 win. Baltimore also took the second game, in which a questionable non-call of runner's interference on the Orioles' B. J. Surhoff in the eighth inning resulted in a Sandy Alomar throwing error. Instead of the inning ending with a double play and a tied score, the Orioles plated three runs and won, 7-4. The Indians returned to Cleveland for Game Three on a Friday afternoon with their backs against the wall.

An Albert Belle grand slam into the autumn dusk broke a 4-4 seventh-inning tie and propelled the Indians to a 9-4 win that extended their season. In another of the most memorable games in Jacobs Field history in Game Four, Indians' pitchers struck out a record twenty-three Orioles, and the Tribe led, 3-2, going into the ninth. One strike away from a deciding Game Five, Jose Mesa gave up a single to Roberto Alomar on a 1-and-2 pitch that scored the tying run and sent the game into extra innings. Alomar then twisted the dagger of irony into the Indians' hearts. Batting against Mesa again to lead off the twelfth, Alomar gulfed a sinker over the center-field wall to send the Orioles to the ALCS against New York. For the first time Jacobs Field was the site of a huge disappointment. In the fall of 1996 a professional baseball team from Baltimore defeated a club from Cleveland in four postseason games, exactly one hundred years after the same thing had happened with the Temple Cup on the line.

By the time the 1997 season began the Indians were a completely different team. In July 1996 Baerga had been traded with Espinoza to the New York Mets in exchange for Jeff Kent and Jose Vizcaino. The Indians had realized Baerga's skills were rapidly deteriorating and opted to trade some power for a better defense. Kent and Vizcaino, along with relief pitcher Julian Tavarez, were then shipped to San Francisco in the offseason for third baseman Matt Williams. A week before spring training ended, Kenny Lofton was traded to Atlanta with Alan Embree for David Justice and Marquis Grissom. Jose Mesa, possibly still scarred from his failure in the 1996 postseason, suddenly lost his confidence as a closer and was replaced in that role by Mike Jackson. But the most dramatic change was the departure of the temperamental but talented Albert Belle, the heart of the offense, who seemed to betray Cleveland fans by turning down a contract extension with the Indians to sign with their divisional rival, the White Sox.

With the franchise in transition, the 1997 Tribe struggled to find an identity and subsequently struggled in the standings. The Indians didn't climb over the .500 mark for good until May 20. Although unchallenged in the division, they still never held more than an eight-game lead, a far cry from the thirty- and 14½-game margins in '95 and '96. The only true model of consistency for the Indians for much of the season was Sandy Alomar, who enjoyed his first completely healthy season since his rookie year of 1990. Alomar—who ripped off a thirty-game hitting streak from late May through early July—would hit .324 with twenty-one homers and eighty-three RBI and was selected to the All-Star Game, held at Jacobs Field. His dream season continued when he hit a game-winning home run in the bottom of the seventh in the midsummer classic. Also that year, just as he did on opening day 1994, he broke up a pitcher's date with destiny. On May 30 at Camden Yards Alomar ended Mike Mussina's bid for a perfect game with a one-out single in the ninth.

Despite Alomar's heroics, the Indians just couldn't seem to find a rhythm all season. They clinched their third consecutive Central crown with a thrilling, come-from-behind 10-9 victory over the defending-champion Yankees at Jacobs Field on September 23. When they were matched with the Yanks for the division series, most figured it was going to be a quick exit for the Tribe. After all, the 1997 team was nowhere near as talented as the 1996 squad that couldn't even get to the ALCS.

The skeptics looked justified after the Indians blew a 5-0 lead in Game One at Yankee Stadium and lost, 8-6. New York jumped on rookie pitcher Jaret Wright, who had started the season at AA Akron, in the first inning of Game Two and led, 3-0. But the Indians rallied back for a 7-5 win to tie the series as it went back to Jacobs Field. David Wells handcuffed the Tribe in Game Three, and the Yankees moved to within one game of appearing in their second straight ALCS with a 6-1 win. They wiggled even closer as they took a 2-1 lead into the bottom of the eighth inning of Game Four and were just four outs away from a series triumph.

Then Sandy Alomar came through once again, this time with a game-tying home run on a 2-and-0 fastball from Mariano Rivera. It would be the start of the most incredible postseason run in the history of Cleveland sports. An Omar Vizquel single off the glove of relief pitcher Ramiro Mendoza in the bottom of the ninth scored Marquis Grissom, and the Indians had forced a Game Five. Wright again took the mound and was solid, and the Indians roared to a 4-0 lead in the fourth. The Yankees narrowed it to 4-3 in the sixth, but could do no more damage until the ninth, when Paul O'Neil rocketed a two-out double off Mesa, who had regained his closer role late in the season. Bernie Williams then flied out to Brian Giles in left to end the game and culminate what to many was the most wonderful moment in Jacobs Field history. The Tribe had defeated its long-time nemesis, the New York Yankees, and was headed for the ALCS in what was supposed to be an off year.

The triumph over New York earned the Indians a rematch with the Orioles, and this time it was Baltimore that held the AL's best record and the Indians whom many felt didn't belong in the playoffs. For the second straight year, Brady Anderson led off a playoff series with the Indians with a homer, and the Orioles took Game One, 3-0. It appeared that all was going as the experts had predicted when Baltimore took a 4-2 lead into the eighth in Game Two, but a three-run home run by Grissom gave the Indians a clutch 5-4 win. It sent the series back to Cleveland for a pair of the wildest games the ballpark would ever see before crowds as energized as have ever attended a Major League Baseball contest.

Another reminder of the Indians' past popped up in Game Three, which pitted veterans Orel Hershiser and Mike Mussina against one another. With the Saturday start time set for just past 4 P.M., the growing late-afternoon shadows at Jacobs Field made the ball difficult to see out of the pitcher's hand. Just as was the case in the first-ever game at Cleveland Stadium when the mound had a backdrop of thousands of white shirts, batters complained they couldn't hit the ball because they simply couldn't see it. As a result Mussina set an LCS record by striking out fifteen Indians, and neither team could mount much of a threat offensively. The Indians finally took a lead in the seventh on an RBI single by Matt Williams, and they appeared to be on their way to a two-games-to-one lead as the score held into the ninth. Then a misplayed fly ball by Grissom allowed Baltimore to tie the contest, and it plunged into extra innings. In the bottom of the twelfth, with Grissom on third and one out, Vizquel attempted to squeeze-bunt home the winning run. He missed the ball, which got by Orioles' catcher Lenny Webster, and Grissom scored to give the Tribe a zany 2-1 win. The wackiness continued the next night as the Indians rallied from a 5-2 deficit, took a 7-5 lead when two runners scored on a wild pitch that never went more than five feet away from home plate, then blew the advantage and went to the bottom of the ninth tied at seven. But Sandy Alomar came through again with a two-out single that scored Manny Ramirez to give the Indians a three-games-to-one lead.

Their World Series tickets were not stamped the next night, however, as the Orioles hung tough with a 4-2 win to send the series back to Baltimore. In Game Six, played on an overcast Wednesday afternoon at Camden Yards, Charles Nagy and Mike Mussina went toe-to-toe in a classic pitchers' duel. Despite several opportunities, the Orioles couldn't break onto the scoreboard, while the Indians only mustered two hits over nine innings. The contest toiled on into the darkness and extra innings, still scoreless, until Cleveland second baseman Tony Fernandez hit a two-out solo home run off Baltimore reliever Armando Benitez in the eleventh. Jose Mesa exorcised some ghosts from the past as he steered the game-ending strike past Roberto Alomar with the tying run on base and two out in the bottom of the inning, and the Indians were once again World Series-bound. This time they would face the Florida Marlins, the National League wild-card entry, who had upset the Atlanta Braves in the NLCS.

After a 7-4 loss in Game One, the Indians bounced back for a 6-1 triumph in the second game to tie the series before returning to cold (and snowy) Jacobs Field for games three through five, a trio of the worst-played games in World Series history. The Marlins took Game Three, 14-11, thanks to a seven-run top of the ninth, which was then followed by a four-run bottom of the ninth by the Indians. Cleveland rebounded with a 10-3 win behind Jaret Wright in Game Four to tie the series, but then watched its bullpen implode in Game Five as the Marlins rallied from a 4-2 deficit to win, 8-7.

The teams returned to Miami for Game Six, which more than made up for the sloppiness of the previous contests. The Indians won, 4-1, behind the arm and the bat of pitcher Chad Ogea, who allowed just one run in five innings and helped his own cause with a single, a double, an RBI, and a run scored. A magnificent defensive play by Omar Vizquel, spearing a sharp Charles Johnson grounder in the eighth, saved at least one run, possibly two, and preserved the win. The Indians, who had won just eighty-six games in the regular season, were now headed for Game Seven of the World Series, and twenty-one-year-old Jaret Wright was to be their starting pitcher.

Wright was magnificent, going 6⅓ innings and allowing just one run. Meanwhile a Tony Fernandez single scored two runs in the third and gave the Indians a lead that would hold until the ninth at 2-1. Jose Mesa came on to save the Tribe's first world championship in forty-nine years but gave up a leadoff single to Moises Alou. After Bobby Bonilla struck out, Charles Johnson smacked an opposite-field single that moved Alou to third. Craig Counsell followed with a game-tying sacrifice fly. The game marched on into the eleventh (just like the first game at Jacobs Field) before Edgar Renteria hit a soft line drive just off the glove of Game Seven starter-turned-reliever Charles Nagy and into center field to score Counsell and give the five-year-old Florida Marlins their first world championship.

Still for a team that had struggled through much of the regular season to come within two outs of the title was impressive and spoke volumes about the foundation the Indians had now laid with John Hart's supervision and also about the impact of Jacobs Field.

The shaky regular season of 1997 was repeated almost exactly in 1998, as the Tribe coasted into the playoffs with an 89-73 mark in a campaign with few true highlights.

One high note came on April 15 when the Mariners and Indians matched up in another memorable contest, but not so much for the game itself. After an inside-the-park home run by the Indians' David Bell in his first at-bat of the season set the tone for a wacky night, the rivalry between Kenny Lofton (re-signed by the Indians as a free agent after one season in Atlanta) and Randy Johnson flared up again. With Lofton leading off the bottom of the third, Johnson's first pitch was a head-high slider that drew some harsh words from the Cleveland center fielder. After the benches and bullpens did their traditional milling around and Johnson was given a warning from the umpires, order was restored, and the at-bat continued. But Johnson's second pitch was a fastball at Lofton's head, and Lofton took off for the mound only to be held back by Seattle catcher Dan Wilson. Sandy Alomar tore out after Johnson from the dugout and had to be restrained by the umpires, while Lou Piniella boiled out of his dugout after Lofton. When the dust settled, Johnson, Lofton, and Alomar had been ejected, and the Mariners went on to win, 5-3.

The Indians would face Johnson in the Kingdome on July 28, just one more time before he was traded to Houston in the National League. This would have been the pitching matchup for Game Seven in the 1995 ALCS. After struggling in domed stadiums throughout his career, Charles Nagy defeated Johnson that night, 4-3, and sent him off to the senior circuit with a good-natured pat on the back.

Another major event of the 1998 season was provided by an opposing player. On June 25 at Jacobs Field, Mark McGwire of the St. Louis Cardinals hit the halfway point in his bid for seventy home runs with a mammoth blast off Dave Burba. The shot hit one of the pillars holding up the scoreboard in left field. This was actually the second time McGwire had reached the scoreboard at Jacobs Field after drilling it on April 30, 1997, while with the Oakland Athletics. That blast was measured at 485 feet, the longest ever hit at the ballpark until Jim Thome hit a 511-foot blast against Kansas City on July 3, 1999, which literally left the ballpark.

After going wire-to-wire (only the seventh major-league team ever to do so) in the hopeless AL Central, the 1998 Indians were matched with the Boston Red Sox, just as they had been three years before. But this series would not prove as easy for the Indians.

Wright was shelled like a peanut in Game One, as the Red Sox triumphed, 11-3, at Jacobs Field. In Game Two Mike Hargrove and starting pitcher Dwight Gooden were ejected in the first inning after disputing a handful of questionable calls by home plate umpire Joe Brinkman. The Tribe overcame the losses and Brinkman's bizarre behavior to even the series at one game apiece with a stirring 9-5 win. The Tribe took Game Three in Fenway, 4-3, but the Red Sox took a 1-0 lead into the eighth inning of Game Four and seemed determined to head to Cleveland for the deciding fifth game. A clutch two-out double by David Justice off Boston closer Tom Gordon scored two runs, and the Indians eliminated the Red Sox, 2-1, and moved on to the ALCS against the Yankees.

New York ripped Wright again and took Game One easily. In Game Two, a key non-call of runner's interference on Cleveland third baseman Travis Fryman resulted in a Yankee error and allowed the game-winning run to score in the twelfth inning. (The non-call became an American tragedy when it hurt the Yankees, but the exact same play had received little national media attention when it cost the Indians Game Two of the 1996 Division Series in Baltimore.) Rookie pitcher Bartolo Colon went the distance in a 6-1 Cleveland win in Game Three at Jacobs Field, giving the Indians a two-games-to-one lead on a team that had won 114 games in the regular season. It didn't last. The Yankees took the next two in Cleveland to go back to New York for Game Six, where they took a 6-0 lead into the fifth. A Jim Thome grand slam brought the Indians back into the contest, but a key error by Vizquel led to three Yankee runs in the sixth, and New York was off to a World Series sweep of the San Diego Padres.

The team seemed reenergized for the 1999 campaign, particularly because of the signing of free-agent second baseman Roberto Alomar, who would finally get a chance to play for Cleveland with his brother. The Indians roared to a 26-9 start, the best in franchise history, but for the third consecutive year they played only a shade above mediocre in the season's second half. They handily won a fifth straight divisional title, and then grabbed a two-games-to-none lead over Boston in their division series rematch. But a banged-up pitching staff was annihilated in the final three games of the series, as the Red Sox scored forty-four runs to win three straight and move on to their first ALCS in nine years. Four days later Mike Hargrove was fired and eventually replaced as manager by batting coach Charlie Manuel. The initial era of success that had started with the opening of Jacobs Field was about to begin its decline.

Just as the opening of the new ballpark clearly marked a new chapter in Indians' history, Richard Jacobs's sale of the team to Larry Dolan after the 1999 season would mark the beginning—or perhaps, more appropriately, the end—of another chapter. Jacobs, who had purchased the team in 1986, had funded one of the greatest financial comebacks in the history of pro sports. He had successfully fought for and received a baseball-only park for his team and turned the Indians from a civic embarrassment into the toast of Cleveland. His leadership and, more appropriately, his free spending were a very big part of the team's transition. No other name would have fit the title of the new ballpark better.

With a new owner and a new manager in place, the 2000 Tribe started the season strong and finished it even stronger. But it was in the middle third of the schedule where permanent damage was done. The Indians hovered around the .500 mark from late June through early August and dug too deep a hole behind the surprising Chicago White Sox. Cleveland managed to get it together in the final two months, winning thirty-eight of its final sixty-one games, and even came up with a clutch sweep of the Toronto Blue Jays on the final weekend of the season, when the Indians were desperately clawing for the wild-card spot. But it was too little, too late. For the first time since 1993 Major League Baseball held its postseason without the Indians, who actually finished with a better record (90-72) than the eventual world-champion New York Yankees (87-74).

By the time the 2001 season began major personnel changes had already taken place. Outfielder David Justice was traded to the Yankees in late June 2000 due to financial constraints, then six young players were dealt away in one day just prior to the trading deadline in a major housecleaning. The team opted not to re-sign free agent Sandy Alomar at season's end, and the longtime Tribe catcher went to the rival White Sox, as had Albert Belle four years earlier.

But perhaps the most telling departure following 2000 was that of Manny Ramirez. The team had attempted to re-sign Ramirez, who was set to become a free agent at the end of the season, to no avail. On the final day of the regular season Ramirez hit a home run in what many figured would be his final at-bat in a Cleveland uniform. It was, as Ramirez agreed to a lucrative (yet not much more so than what the Indians had proposed) offer with the Boston Red Sox.

With these changes, plus the fact that the team hadn't made the playoffs for the first time in six seasons, it was only natural that Jacobs Field's incredible string of consecutive sellouts came to a close early in 2001 at 455, a major-league record. But attendance was still healthy for the Indians, especially as the 2001 season wore on.

The Indians plugged the Ramirez loss somewhat with the signing of power-hitting free-agent outfielder Juan Gonzalez to a one-year contract prior to the 2001 season, but it was fairly obvious to most fans that Gonzalez would not stick around. He didn't, bolting back to Texas after hitting thirty-five home runs and driving in 140 RBI for Cleveland.

Still, led by Gonzalez, veteran outfielder Ellis Burks, Roberto Alomar, young pitchers Bartolo Colon and C. C. Sabathia, plus old reliables Jim Thome and Omar Vizquel, the Indians had one last title run left in them. The 2001 Tribe overcame a five-game deficit to the Minnesota Twins at the All-Star break and wound up winning its sixth AL Central crown in seven years with a 91-71 record. It seems appropriate that this final upbeat season that marked the tail end of a long run of success came to a close against the same team in which it had begun—the Seattle Mariners.

The 2001 Mariners had set an American League record with 116 victories in the regular season, and many expected them to simply blow past the aging Tribe in the best-of-five division series. But the Indians surprised even their own fans by taking two of the first three games, including a 17-2 stomping of baseball's best team at Jacobs Field in Game Three. Back at the Jake for Game Four, the Tribe snuck a 1-0 lead into the seventh inning and were in a position to end the series then and there and complete one of the biggest upsets in baseball history. But key errors and a lack of clutch pitching allowed the Mariners to plate six runs in their final three at-bats to win the game, tie the series, and send it back to Seattle for the deciding Game Five.

But many Cleveland fans knew that the Indians needn't have even made the trip. Seven-and-a-half years after a win over the Seattle Mariners began a nearly decade-long string of excellence, a loss to the Seattle Mariners drew that era to a close. The Tribe's bats were helpless against Seattle pitcher Jamie Moyer for the second time in the series, and the Mariners won, 3-1, advancing to the American

League Championship Series. No surprise to baseball pragmatists, Seattle's 116 wins didn't mean a thing the following week as they were handled by the big-market, big-money Yankees in five games.

Two weeks after the 2001 season ended, John Hart stepped down as the Indians' general manager, as he had announced he would early in the year. Taking over was his assistant, Mark Shapiro, who would have a tough act to follow.

Certainly many fans grew tired of Hart's inability to acquire a top-notch pitching ace that could have put the Indians over the top in the late 1990s and turned them into an unquestioned dynasty. Some of Hart's later deals—which sent away young players with potential in exchange for older veterans who might have helped the Indians win a championship right away—were incredibly damaging in the long run. Youngsters such as Sean Casey, Richie Sexson, Jeromy Burnitz, Brian Giles, David Bell, Steve Karsay, Alex Ramirez, Enrique Wilson, and Danny Graves all passed through Cleveland in the late 1990s on their way to more playing time and in some cases very prosperous careers elsewhere.

Hart knew that the Indians' window of opportunity would only stay open for a relatively short period of time. After sacrificing the present for the future in the early 1990s he knew he had to do the exact opposite in the second half of the decade to keep that window open. In retrospect, he was ultimately unsuccessful.

But it would be impulsive to judge Hart solely on the fact that he never was able to capture a World Series. When he took over as general manager in 1991 the Indians hadn't appeared in the postseason in thirty-seven years. When he left they'd made the playoffs six of the previous seven seasons, won two pennants, and came within two outs of a world championship. From 1994 through 2001 the Indians compiled a record of 718-509. That's a winning percentage of .585, which translates to an average of ninety-five victories per year. Only two teams—the New York Yankees and Atlanta Braves—held better records during this period. Only a fool would call Hart a failure.

Still with Hart serving as the general manager in Texas beginning in 2002, Shapiro and Dolan would have to wade through the results of some of Hart's now-or-never deals. Thus, with Dolan tightening the franchise's purse strings, the Indians became an almost entirely different team in the 2001–2002 offseason. By opening day 2002 only three players remained on the Cleveland roster who were there when Jacobs Field opened: Charles Nagy, Jim Thome, and Omar Vizquel.

The team waved goodbye to free agents Kenny Lofton, Dave Burba, Marty Cordova, and Gonzalez. Then in December 2001 the Indians traded away second baseman Roberto Alomar to the New York Mets, primarily in exchange for outfielder Matt Lawton and top minor-league prospects Alex Escobar and Jerrod

Riggan. While many fans bemoaned the deal at the time, calling for Shapiro's head for trading away the picked-apart team's only remaining bona-fide star, the similarities to this trade and the Joe Carter deal in 1989 that brought Carlos Baerga and Sandy Alomar to Cleveland are too obvious to dismiss. That trade was the centerpiece of the Indians' late 1990s renaissance. Only time will tell if the Roberto Alomar trade will spark another. If nothing else, the Indians wisely dealt Alomar just before his career took a down turn. After hitting .266 with the Mets in 2002 (his lowest average since his rookie year in 1988), then just .253 in sixty-seven games the following year, New York traded him to the Chicago White Sox for three minor-leaguers in July 2003.

But the Alomar trade paled in comparison to the heartbreak Indians fans felt when Jim Thome abandoned the team following the 2002 season. After spending nine seasons as part of the Indians' nucleus, becoming the franchise's all-time leader in home runs (334) and walks (997), Thome opted for greener pastures as a free agent in Philadelphia. Like Albert Belle and Manny Ramirez before him, Thome joined an ever-growing fraternity of legendary sluggers who, for better or worse, were adored by Cleveland fans and enjoyed a wonderful career with the Indians—only to toss it aside for more money elsewhere.

While many fans have been heartbroken and frustrated with the Indians coming so close to a pair of world championships, it's doubtful any would have preferred the team remain in its pre-Jacobs Field quagmire. Anyone would agree that a handful of playoff berths and near misses are far better than three decades of seeing the Indians eliminated from the pennant race by Independence Day. Because of the stability that Jacobs Field brought, for the first time in a generation, fans knew that they could count on seeing a playoff-caliber baseball team year-in and year-out in downtown Cleveland.

The Seattle Mariners, by contrast, were really no better than the Indians were, on paper, at the beginning of 1994. But over the next six seasons, despite having arguably the best hitter (Ken Griffey Jr.) and the best pitcher (Randy Johnson) in baseball, the Mariners were disappointingly inconsistent.

After a 49-63 season in 1994, the Mariners got hot at the right time and managed a spot in the American League Championship Series against the Indians in 1995—but that could be attributed more to an August-September nosedive by the California Angels and a three-game vacation by the Yankees in the division series. A young shortstop named Alex Rodriguez surfaced in 1996 and eased the pain of the Omar Vizquel trade by winning the Rookie of the Year Award. But the Mariners still dropped to 85-76, 2½ games out of the wild-card spot, before bouncing back the following year. The 1997 Mariners won ninety games and took their second AL West crown but were quickly dispatched by Baltimore in the division series.

The team moved into its new stadium, Safeco Field, in 1999, but the new location didn't offer any immediate turnaround as Jacobs Field had. After another losing record to open the new ballpark, Ken Griffey Jr. was traded to the Cincinnati Reds under circumstances similar to Johnson, who was traded to Houston in 1998. In 2000 free-agent Alex Rodriguez departed for Texas, which offered an outrageous amount of money.

Once Johnson, Griffey, and Rodriguez departed, however, the Mariners finally became an elite team. After a ninety-one-win season and an appearance in the ALCS in 2000, Seattle won 116 in 2001, baseball's highest win total in ninety-five years. Instead of relying on a handful of superstars, the Mariners loaded up on well-balanced young talent—much like the Indians had a few seasons earlier.

While the Mariners could point to the departures of their All-Star trio as the transactions that set up an extended run of success, the 1994–2001 Indians needed to look no further than their own infield. Certainly the Joe Carter trade set the tone for the Tribe to climb from embarrassing to respectable, but another deal was just as instrumental in helping the Indians take the next step.

The Omar Vizquel–Felix Fermin trade on December 20, 1993, symbolized a dramatic change for the Indians, not only on the field but also in the front office. While Fermin went on to hit a career-best .317 with Seattle in 1994, he hit just .195 in 73 games in 1995. With the emergence of Alex Rodriguez in 1996, Fermin's stay in Seattle was shortened, and his career came to a quiet conclusion with the Chicago Cubs.

With Rodriguez waiting in the wings, it wasn't as if Vizquel would have played his entire career in Seattle. But in retrospect, the Mariners should have received, whether from the Indians or another team, much more for him than just Fermin and Reggie Jefferson. And what they could have received might have pushed them over the hump in the late 1990s and early 2000s.

Vizquel seemed to get better with each passing season. After hitting .273 in 1994 and .266 in 1995 (incidentally, Vizquel and Paul Sorrento were the only two Cleveland starters not to hit .300 that year), Vizquel batted a then-career-best .297 in 1996 and stayed above .280 each of the next two years. In 1999 Vizquel had the best season of his career, batting .333 with 191 hits, 112 runs, 36 doubles, 42 steals, and 66 RBI, all career-bests at the time. That year he was the Indians' best clutch hitter on a team that became the first to score more than a thousand runs since the 1950 Red Sox. Vizquel went on to hit .287 in 2000, and although he dropped to .255 in 2001 he still compiled a .973 fielding percentage, won his ninth straight Gold Glove, and hit .435 in the division series. As his role changed to one of veteran leadership, Vizquel bounced back to hit .275 in 2002 with a downright Ruthian fourteen home runs, while knocking in a career-best seventy-two RBI. In his first ten years with the Indians, the first ten years of the Jacobs Field era, Vizquel hit .282 and never had a fielding percentage lower than .971.

As Vizquel helped lead the Indians into the twenty-first century, Fermin was doing the same. Two years after his 1996 retirement, he took over as manager of the Indians' Dominican Summer League Team, helping develop the younger talent in the organization.

With Thome a Phillie and Nagy wrapping up his steady-as-she-goes career, the only Indian remaining on the 2003 opening-day lineup who had played in the first game at Jacobs Field was, it seems appropriate to say, Omar Vizquel. In the first ten years of Jacobs Field, as the Indians once again joined the upper echelon of baseball, there had been many more glamorous, more feared players in the Cleveland lineup, but none better symbolized the steady progression and abounding enthusiasm of the new Cleveland Indians than Omar Vizquel, who must go down as one of the best—and most important—players in franchise history. In the history of trades made by the Cleveland Indians, Fermin-for-Vizquel had to be one of the best. It seems like more than just simple coincidence that this beauty of an exchange was showcased in the first game at the brand-new ballpark. This circumstance, like many others on April 4, 1994, made it clear that this was a whole different brand of Cleveland Indians baseball.

The Jacobs Field–era of success for the Indians had to do with more than just the park's physical reality. While baseball realists were quick to point out that the only reason the Indians were able to compete each season was because of the revenue that the still-new Jacobs Field provided, the park represented more than a silver collection plate passed around the city of Cleveland each summer. In an era when the decks are stacked in favor of teams in large media markets like New York, Atlanta, and Los Angeles, Jacobs Field provided a way to keep Cleveland, a medium-sized market, in the loop. Starting with the very first game at Jacobs Field, the park symbolized the franchise's own field of dreams and made possible the latest dramatic baseball renaissance in Northeast Ohio. Not only did it result in the longest consecutive sellout streak in the history of baseball, it also proved to even the most pessimistic disbeliever that miracles are possible—even a franchise as hopeless as the Cleveland Indians had been could turn itself around with proper planning and execution.

Even more important than the business and financial side of baseball, the Indians' opening game at Jacobs Field was the first in a long line of incredible comebacks, as the Indians became baseball's version of the Kardiac Kids throughout the remainder of the 1990s and into the next decade.

"That game was so important to this club," John Hart said of the opening day game in a team video about the creation of Jacobs Field. "One, we felt we had a club that was ready to break through, and two, moving into our own ballpark and setting our own turf (proved) that we were going to be a tough club to beat. I think that propelled us toward a quality '94 season and I think that was the first step that got our guys believing that the extra innings belonged to the Indians."

Of the Tribe's first 140 victories at Jacobs Field, forty came in the team's final at-bat. Of the first 184, 103 were come-from-behind wins. Cleveland was 8-3 in extra-inning games in 1994 and 12-0 in 1995, and fifteen of those combined twenty victories took place at Jacobs Field. They also won a total of forty-six games in their last at-bat in 1995 and 1996. In 1999 the Indians became the first team in major-league history to come back from eight-run deficits three times to win games—all at Jacobs Field.

But those were simply preludes to the greatest comeback in the history of Major League Baseball. On a sultry Sunday night in August 2001 the Indians rallied from a 14-2 deficit in the seventh inning to defeat, again appropriately, the Seattle Mariners, 15-14, in eleven innings at Jacobs Field. The decades of strife for Cleveland baseball fans and the early innings of many games at Jacobs Field seem to parallel one another: if the team just hung in there and stayed positive, sooner or later good things would happen. Almost all of these thrillers, especially those in the early years, ended with an Indian crossing home plate and his teammates pounding him on the batting helmet as hard as they could—a tradition that began with Sandy Alomar's love tap of Wayne Kirby. And all of it—the six division titles, the two pennants, the franchise's civic redemption—began with a 4-3, eleven-inning victory over the Seattle Mariners on April 4, 1994.

Had the Indians lost that game they still would have gone on to success in the coming seasons. Without that opening-day victory, though, the break in Indians' history would not have been as clear. With one game, a franchise that had played tens of thousands over nearly a century was changed forever.

"You can say so many things about this game," Candy Maldonado said in the locker room following that first contest at Jacobs Field. "But finally, when it's over, it just was a beautiful ballgame."

And the beginning of a beautiful relationship.

BIBLIOGRAPHY

Alexander, Charles C. *Our Game: An American Baseball History.* New York: Henry Holt, 1991.

The Baseball Encyclopedia: The Complete and Definitive Record of Major League Baseball. 10th ed. New York: Macmillan, 1996.

Dyer, Bob. "The Indians' New Field of Dreams." *Beacon: The Magazine of the Beacon Journal,* March 27, 1994, 4–8, 15, 20.

Feller, Bob, and Bill Gilbert. *Now Pitching: Bob Feller.* New York: Carol, 1990.

Feinstein, John. *Play Ball: The Life and Troubled Times of Major League Baseball.* New York: Random House, 1995.

Filichia, Peter. *Professional Baseball Franchises: From the Abbeville Athletics to the Zanesville Indians.* New York: Facts on File, 1993.

Fimrite, Ron. *A Series for the Fans.* San Francisco, Calif.: Woodford, 1995.

Hodermarsky, Mark, ed. *The Cleveland Sports Legacy Since 1945.* Cleveland, Ohio: Cleveland Landmarks, 1991.

Jenkins, Bruce. *A Series for the Americas.* San Francisco, Calif.: Woodford, 1997.

Kelly, Thomas, and Marc Jaffe. *The Summer of 95.* N.p.: Archives, 1995.

Kerr, Don. *Opening Day: All Major League Baseball Season Opening Games, by Team, 1876–1998.* Jefferson, N.C.: McFarland, 1999.

LaBlanc, Michael L. *Hot Dogs, Heroes, and Hooligans.* Detroit, Mich.: Visible Ink, 1994.

Pluto, Terry. *Burying the Curse: How the Indians became the Best Team in Baseball.* Akron, Ohio: Beacon Journal Publishing, 1995.

———. *The Curse of Rocky Colavito: A Loving Look at a Thirty-Year Slump.* New York: Simon and Schuster, 1994.

———. *Our Tribe: A Baseball Memoir.* New York: Simon and Schuster, 1999.

Rhodes, Greg, and John Erardi. *Big Red Dynasty: How Bob Howsam and Sparky Anderson Built the Big Red Machine.* Cincinnati, Ohio: Road West, 1997.

Robinson, Frank, and Barry Stanback. *Extra Innings.* New York: McGraw-Hill, 1988.

Schneider, Russell. *The Cleveland Indians Encyclopedia.* Philadelphia, Pa.: Temple Univ. Press, 1996.

———. *The Glorious Indian Summer of 1995.* Cleveland, Ohio: Russell Schneider, 1995.

———. *The Unfulfilled Indian Summer of 1996.* Cleveland, Ohio: Russell Schneider, 1996.

Thorn, John, et al., eds. *Total Indians.* New York: Penguin, 1996.

Thorn, John, Pete Palmer, and Michael Gershman, eds. *Total Baseball: The Official Encyclopedia of Major League Baseball.* Vol. 4. New York: Penguin, 1995.

Toman, James A., and Gregory G. Deegan. *Cleveland Stadium: The Last Chapter.* Cleveland, Ohio: Cleveland Landmarks, 1997.

Torry, Jack. *Endless Summers: The Fall and Rise of the Cleveland Indians.* South Bend,
Ind.: Diamond, 1995.

PERIODICALS

Akron Beacon Journal, April 5, 1994, April 16, 1998, April 13, 2000.

Cleveland Indians Media Guides: 1993–2000.

Cleveland Plain Dealer, May 1–2, 1891, July 2–3, 1931, August 1, 1932, April 16–17, 1940, April
18–20, 1960, April 8–9, 1975, May 9, 1990, April 11–12, 1992, March 31, 1994, April 5, 1994.

Cleveland Press, August 1, 1932, April 17–19, 1940.

VIDEOCASSETTES

Cleveland Rocks. VHS. Directed by Rich Domich. Major League Baseball Productions, 1995.

A Cleveland Sock-Sess Story. VHS. Cleveland: Cleveland Indians, 1997.

Indians Baseball at Jacobs Field: Just the Beginning. VHS. Produced by Michael T. Lehr.
Cleveland: Cleveland Indians, 1994.

SRO: Still Rockin' On. VHS. Produced by Steve Warren. Cleveland: Cleveland Indians, 1996.

Wahoo! What a Finish! VHS. Directed by Rich Domich. Major League Baseball Productions,
1995.